HORRIBLE

D0527686

GRUESOME
GREAT HOUSES

Terry Deary Illustr

■SCHOLAS

LANCASHIRE COUNTY LIBRARY

30118134950561

Lancashire Library Services	
30118134950561	
PETERS	J941DEA
£6.99	20-Oct-2017
NMO	

Euston House, 24 Eversholt Street,
London NW1 1DB, UK

A division of Scholastic Ltd
London ~ New York ~ Toronto ~ Sydney ~ Auckland
Mexico City ~ New Delhi ~ Hong Kong

Published in the UK by Scholastic Ltd, 2017

Text © Terry Deary, 2017
Cover illustration © Martin Brown 2017, line and colour by Rob Davis
Illustrations copyright © Martin Brown, Mike Phillips, 2017

All rights reserved

ISBN 978 1407 17872 1

Printed and bound in the UK by CPI Group (UK) Ltd, Croydon, CR0 4YY

2 4 6 8 10 9 7 5 3 1

The rights of Terry Deary, Martin Brown and Mike Phillips to be identified as the author and
illustrators of this work respectively has been asserted by them in accordance with the
Copyright, Designs and Patents Act, 1988.

This book is sold subject to the condition that it shall not, by way of trade or otherwise be lent,
resold, hired out, or otherwise circulated without the publisher's prior consent in any form or
binding other than that in which it is published and without a similar condition, including this
condition, being imposed upon the subsequent purchaser.

Papers used by Scholastic Children's Books are made from wood grown in sustainable forests.

www.scholastic.co.uk

Contents

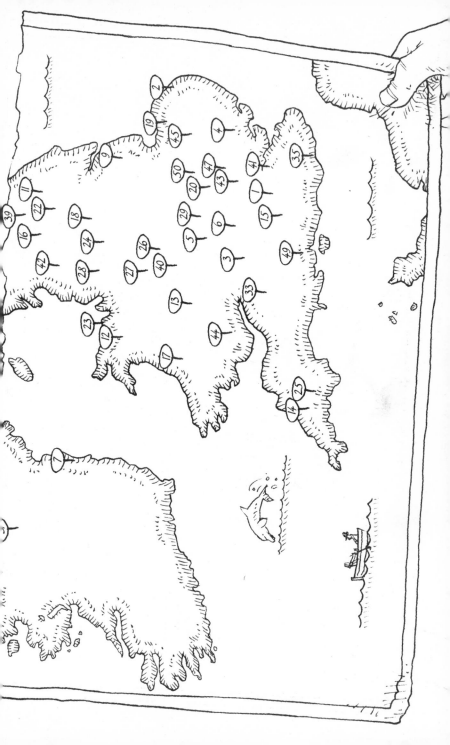

INTRODUCTION

It is a wild and stormy night ... it usually is in horror stories. A group of travellers set out on a journey into the unknown. Why? I don't know. It's unknown.

The travellers are lost on the twisting roads through the mountains. That serves them right for using their map as an umbrella while they ran to the car.

A wise man once said...

(Yes, I agree. He wasn't all THAT wise.)

Anyway, the car breaks down. The storm rages.

Hellhounds howl. So do the owls … or h-owls. Lightning flashes and in the light of the flash they see…

Fat chance. You KNOW it is going to be a night of terror for them.

How do you know? Because they couldn't break down outside your Aunty Maureen's bungalow by the seaside. Or a cosy tavern in a cute little village. Not even outside your own slightly scruffy front door. Oh no. They have to break down outside a huge house. It will have dozens of rooms, crooked corridors, secret passages and be owned by evil people.

But that's just in stories, isn't it?

What is it about great houses that make them so scary? Are there any gruesome great houses in the real world? Houses full of horrors and potty people?

Of course there are. At least there used to be. What you need is a list of these horrible historical places so you can visit them when it is NOT a dark and stormy night with hellhounds and owls' howls.

Unless you want to be scared half to death, of course.

NO THANKS, MATE

1. DEEPDENE HOUSE
Surrey, England

In the early 1800s Lord Hope lived at the hillside manor, Deepdene House.

He liked the view from the front but couldn't see the view from the other side of the hill.

So what did he do? Dug a tunnel from the house through the hill. It cost a fortune but he had a fortune to spend. Wouldn't it have been easier just to walk to the top of the hill, Lord Hope?

Terrible tale

One night a servant told him there was someone lurking in the grounds. Those grounds stretched for 12 miles ... yes, miles.

Lord Hope set off with his sword and hunting dog and caught the lurking man. As the man made a run for it his lordship thrust his sword into him.

Day dawned and Lord Hope saw the dying man was...

The ghost of Lord Hope wanders, weeping, through the place where the gardens stood. You'd expect that, I suppose. But there is also an evil black dog that prowls the night.

There now

The house was flattened by British Rail in 1967. The nearby Betchworth Park golf course is now haunted by that black dog, of course. (Golf course ... of course? Get it? Oh, never mind.)

Accidents happen in the area and strange things are seen.

The family mausoleum – burial house – was overgrown. Plans to repair it were completed in 2016.

2. CROMER HALL
Norfolk, England

The world's most famous storybook detective is Sherlock Holmes, from the books by Arthur Conan Doyle. And one of his most popular stories is *The Hound of the Baskervilles*. It is the tale about the murder of Sir Charles Baskerville. He died with a look of horror on his face and the footprints of a gigantic hound nearby. He had been frightened to death.

Where did Arthur Conan Doyle get his idea from? Conan Doyle went on holiday to Cromer in Norfolk and visited

Cromer Hall. The owner of the hall, Benjamin Cabell, told a tale of terror about his ancestor, Richard Cabell.

In 1677 the cruel Richard Cabell lived at Brook Manor House in Devon. He bullied his wife terribly.

Cabell followed her and stabbed her to death. But her faithful hound attacked him and tore out his throat.

One night she ran away across the moors.

On the night of his death black hounds breathing fire and smoke raced over the moor and surrounded Brook Manor House, howling.

Conan Doyle used the real Cromer Hall as the idea for Baskerville Hall in his story, set in Devonshire. But there is another creepier tale about the book and the writer.

It is said Conan Doyle wrote *The Hound of the Baskervilles* with the help of a friend called Bertram Robinson. The book became a great success and made a lot of money. Of course Robinson deserved a share of that money.

Instead of sharing the money Conan Doyle poisoned Robinson.

The tale is probably as potty as *The Hound of the Baskervilles* ... but it is true that Robinson died young. He was just 36. Was he sick or was he poisoned? It's a case for Sherlock Holmes.

Did you know?

Even though the Richard Cabell murder and the writing of *The Hound of the Baskervilles* happened in Devon, the Cabell family cannot escape the curse of the hound. A phantom black hound appears wherever they live, even in Cromer Hall in Norfolk.

In Norfolk there are many legends of a 'Black Shuck' – a terrible hound that brings terror to parts of the county. It is the Devil's dog sent from hell. Anybody who looks into the eyes of the hound has just one year to live.

There now

The Cabell family still live at Cromer Hall. It isn't open to the public.

3. HIGHCLERE CASTLE
Hampshire, England

There are a lot of dead dogs around these gruesome great houses.

The Earl of Carnarvon had a dog. He left the dog at Highclere Castle when he went off to Egypt to look for ancient mummies' tombs.

NOT A LOT OF TREES IN EGYPT. I'M BETTER OFF AT HIGHCLERE, AREN'T I?

In 1922 the earl found one of the richest historical treasures ever – the tomb of Egyptian King Tutankhamun.

But Carnarvon never got to enjoy it. He was bitten on the face by a mosquito. Just as the bite started to heal, the scab came off when he was shaving. The cut got infected and gave him blood poisoning. He fell ill and died. He was 56.

THEN the wild stories started…

A writer, Marie Corelli, said it served him right for breaking into the dead king's tomb...

I own a rare book which says a terrible punishment follows anyone who breaks into a sealed tomb. The book names 'secret poisons in boxes'. Those who touch them shall suffer.

No one has ever seen this book. Was she a Corel-liar?

Then another story said Carter had found a message in the tomb that read...

Death Shall Come on Swift Wings to Him Who Disturbs the Peace of the King

There was no such message but people believed it. Another whopping lie the size of a pyramid.

There were more tales told:

❀ When the earl died there was a power failure and all the lights throughout Cairo went out.

❀ Carnarvon's son reported that back at Highclere Castle the earl's favourite dog howled and suddenly dropped dead.

AND I THOUGHT I WAS SAFE STAYING HOME.
I HOPE THEY HAVE TREES IN HEAVEN

Every time something bad happened around the Tutankhamun treasure people cried, 'It's the curse.'

🌸 Lord Westbury's son had worked on the tomb. Lord Westbury killed himself by jumping from a building. He left a note that read:

> I really cannot stand any more horrors and hardly see what good I am going to do here, so I am making my exit.

🌸 Back in Egypt the chief digger, Howard Carter, went home one night and found his pet canary had been eaten by a snake. ('Not true,' the budgie might have tweeted.)

Most of these stories were nonsense. Highclere Castle has been quite a lucky great house. When it started to crumble the family needed millions of pounds to repair it. Along came a television company and made a popular series called *Downton Abbey*. Visitors paid to see the famous house and their money saved it.

But Lord Carnarvon and his dog are still dead.

There now

Highclere Castle is open to the public at certain times throughout the year.

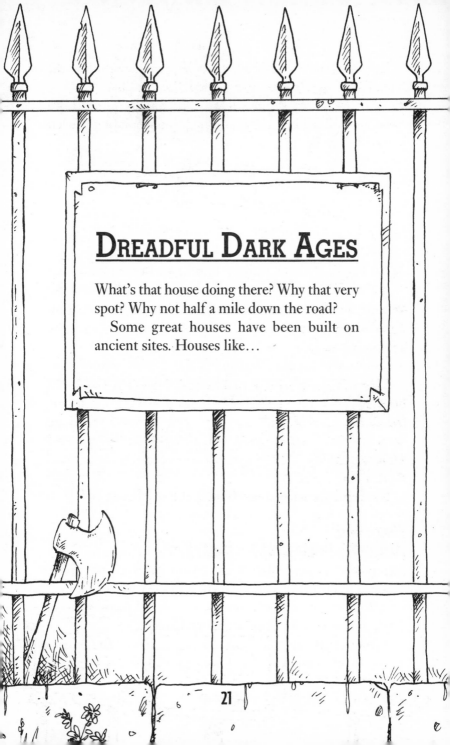

DREADFUL DARK AGES

What's that house doing there? Why that very spot? Why not half a mile down the road?

Some great houses have been built on ancient sites. Houses like…

4. LAYER MARNEY TOWER
Essex, England

The house at Layer Marney Tower was built in 1166, then turned into a great house in 1520 when Henry VIII ruled. But the site was chosen back in the days of the Anglo-Saxons and the Vikings.

In Saxon times Layer Marney hill was a great lookout spot.

The Vikings had struck at the Battle of Maldon in 991. It was a tragic tale of one Saxon's stupidity.

Brithnoth the brave (but batty)

Brithnoth was an old, but brave, Saxon warrior. The Vikings landed on the little island of Northey in the River Blackwater near Maldon, Essex. Brithnoth's army faced them from the bank of the river, across the shallow water.

First the Vikings told Brithnoth they wanted the Saxons to pay them to go away. An ancient poem told the tale…

*PAY US WITH GREAT BAGS OF GOLD
AND WE WILL LET YOU LIVE ON HERE*

Bold Brithnoth replied…

*THE ONLY PAY THAT YOU WILL GET
IS WITH OUR SWORD BLADES AND OUR SPEARS*

Tough talk. The island of Northey was joined to the shore by a strip of mud at low tide. As the Vikings tried to cross, Brithnoth's men cut them down.

The Vikings said…

*WE CANNOT CROSS, WE'LL ALL BE DROWNED.
MAY WE SAIL ACROSS TO SOLID GROUND?*

A wise old warrior would say, 'No.' In fact only a bird-brained idiot would say, 'Yes.'

Brithnoth said, 'Yes.'

Brithnoth was a brave and heroic man. He was soon a brave and heroic corpse as the Vikings cut him and his men to pieces.

But at least he tried to fight back. His king, King Æthelred, simply said…

PAY THEM

Did you know?

🌟 The gatehouse at Layer Marney is the tallest in England. It's a record.

🌟 Henry VIII stayed at Layer Marney in 1522, even though it wasn't finished – he stayed at a building site.

🌟 Lord Marney built the house. His ghost stalks the staircase, dressed in a full suit of armour. It seems he is annoyed that his great house was never finished.

🌟 Lord Marney's ghost has also been seen riding his horse through the grounds, still in that armour.

🌟 In 1835 the tower was owned by Quintin Dick, who became Member of Parliament for Maldon. People voted for him because he paid them to. He paid them more than any other MP of his time. Another record.

🌟 Layer Marney suffered damage from The Great Colchester Earthquake of 1884.

There now

The tower and gardens are open to the public at certain times of the year.

5. BLENHEIM PALACE
Oxfordshire, England

King Henry I built a hunting lodge near to where Blenheim Palace stands today. He had seven miles of walls built around it to make a park. Inside the walls were lions and other exotic animals that he could ride out and kill.

Henry I's grandson, King Henry II, then turned the lodge into a palace. It had fine gardens and deep inside these gardens he built a second little house for his girlfriend, Rosamund Clifford – or 'Fair Rosamund'.

IF THE LIONS HAD LUNCHED ON HER THEN IT WOULD HAVE BEEN UNFAIR FOR ROSAMUND

But one story says she met an even nastier end. King Henry II was married to the fierce Eleanor and Eleanor wanted Fair Rosamund fairly dead. Henry built a maze around Rosamund's little house and he was the only one who knew how to get in.

One day Eleanor tied a silk thread to the heel of her husband's boot so she would know the way too. She waited till Henry was gone and slipped in. When she met Fair Rosamund she gave her the choice…

Other tales said she was roasted alive between two fires or stabbed and left to bleed to death in a bath of scalding water. Grim tales but just legends and not true.

Blenheim tales

🌸 King Henry VIII had a daughter, Mary, who took the throne of England. Mary was sure her younger sister, Elizabeth, had plotted a rebellion. So Elizabeth was locked up at Blenheim Palace. Of course, Elizabeth went on to become Queen Elizabeth I.

🌸 In 1802 Blenheim was visited by the famous Admiral Lord Nelson – the man who led the British warships against the French and won. The duke who owned the palace didn't want to meet him. He sent servants out to give Nelson tea in the park. The admiral was furious.

🌸 Around 1900 many great houses were falling down as no one had the money to repair them. In 1895 Charles, Duke of

Marlborough, solved the problem. He married a rich American, Consuela. She got the title Duchess, he got millions of pounds. Consuela wasn't happy about being married off. She said her family locked her in a room till she agreed.

🌸 In World War I (1914–1918) there were thousands of wounded soldiers and not enough hospitals. A lot of great houses like Blenheim were turned into hospitals. They treated a lot of gruesome injuries.

🌸 In World War II (1939–1945) many schools were moved to the countryside to escape the enemy bombers. 400 boys were evacuated to Blenheim and used the great rooms as classrooms – the boys even had lessons in the bathrooms.

🌸 The boys moved out and in 1940 Blenheim Palace was used by the British spy service MI5.

There now

Rosamund's house was pulled down when Blenheim Palace was built. In the park at Blenheim there is a pool called 'Fair Rosamund's Well'. Blenheim Palace is open to the public all year round.

FAIR ROSAMUND'S WELL

IS SHE?

6. CLIVEDEN
Buckinghamshire, England

Another girlfriend who made trouble at a great house was Anna, the Countess of Shrewsbury. She lived at Cliveden with her lover, George Villiers, the 2nd Duke of Buckingham (1628-1687).

George Villiers had led a dangerous life. When he was just seven months old his dad, the 1st Duke of Buckingham, was assassinated – stabbed to death in a Portsmouth pub called The Greyhound.

THERE ARE A LOT OF DANGEROUS HOUNDS IN THIS BOOK

His killer was a man called John Felton and a lot of people agreed that George's dad deserved to die. A poet wrote...

The Duke is dead, and we are free of strife,
By Felton's hand that took away his life.

29

Felton was hanged, but it wasn't wise to say you liked the assassin. One man who cheered for Felton was fined £2,000 and told he'd have his ears cut off. (The king spared his ears).

King Charles I had been a great friend of George's daggered dad. Charles went to war with Parliament (the Roundheads) in the English Civil War. George Villiers fought for the king and saw his brother die in a battle.

In another battle George escaped after fighting six Roundhead opponents, his back against an oak tree.

Charles I lost the war and was beheaded. (That's not so painful as having your ears cut off but still ruins your day.)

When Charles II came to the throne Villiers was still finding trouble. He had an argument with the Marquess of Dorchester. How did he upset Dorchester?

a) Stuck his tongue out at Dorchester

b) Cut out Dorchester's tongue

c) Pulled Dorchester's wig off

Answer (c)
Yes, these great lords fought like schoolboys in the playground.

Lord Shrewsbury also squabbled with Buckingham about the lord's wife, but this time they squabbled with swords. Dangerous.

They say that Countess Shrewsbury – the one they had been fighting over – disguised herself as a page-boy so she could watch the duel. When George won she gave him a big hug – while his shirt was still soaked in her husband's blood.

Did you know?

England has never had a King Fred. But it should have had. Prince Frederick was the son of King George II and would take the throne when his dad died.

But one day in 1751 he played in a cricket match at Cliveden. He was hit in the chest and died.

Nobody liked the rest of the royal family, so a sad (but silly) poem was written after Fred died.

Here lies poor Fred who was alive and is dead,
Had it been his father I had much rather,
Had it been his sister nobody would have missed her,
Had it been his brother, still better than another.
But since it is Fred who was alive and is dead,
There is no more to be said.

Did you also know?

George Villiers is said to haunt the ladies' toilets in the Cock & Bottle pub in York. George had a laboratory there where he tried to turn lead into gold.

In modern times a strange man was caught spying on a lady having a shower at the Cock & Bottle. The landlord chased the man who ran upstairs. When they reached the attic the stranger had vanished. He looked a lot like George, 1st Duke of Buckingham. Was it naughty George?

YOU OFTEN SEE SPIRITS IN PUBS

There now
Cliveden is now a hotel where you can stay if you have the money.

7. HOWTH CASTLE
County Dublin, Ireland

Women in history could be cruel and tough. Grace O'Malley (1530–1603) was born into a family of Irish sailors and traders ... with a touch of piracy when they felt like it.

Grace wanted to be a sailor like the rest of her family. But her father told the young girl:

YOUR LONG HAIR WOULD TANGLE IN THE ROPES

Grace was furious. She dressed like a boy and hacked her hair till it was short like a sailor's. Sorted. She told her father she was ready to sail with him. Her family laughed and gave her a new nickname: Gráinne Mhaol (Grace the Bald). But gruesome Grace's temper could be deadly. An ancient jester told this tale...

33

The wind whipped off the Irish Sea and tugged at the cloak of the woman on the horse. 'Not far now,' she called over the wail of the wind. 'Howth Castle in half a mile will give us shelter for the night.'

The woman looked strong as a bear under that great grey cloak and her face was hard as the rocks on the road. The man nodded, shivered inside his leather jerkin and spurred his tired horse up the hill.

Howth Castle towered above them and the massive walls sheltered them from the wind. As the woman reached the mighty oak gates a servant in a beetle-black suit scuttled across the castle yard. The woman smiled at him. 'Good evening,' she said.

The servant wrinkled his pale face in a sour snarl. 'Stand back. Stand back, I say. I need to close the gates. It's sunset. Have to close the gates.'

The woman raised a hand as the servant grasped the gate. 'I am Grace O'Malley. I am captain of one of Queen Elizabeth's ships. I come to visit the Lord of Howth.'

The servant pulled back his bloodless lips in a broken-toothed sneer. 'Well, you're too late. His lordship has started dinner. It's more than my job's worth to disturb him now.'

With a flick of his frail wrists the servant swung the door shut and Grace's startled horse reared up. By the time her bodyguard in the leather jerkin had helped her calm it, the bars had been slammed into place.

The woman's weather-worn face was pale with fury. She turned and walked her horse down the hill towards Dublin bay.

'A fine welcome, Mallen,' she said. 'We must repay the Lord of Howth's kindness some day.'

'Yes, ma'am,' Mallen murmured but his words were whisked away by the biting wind. They bent their heads into the stinging rain and didn't see the horsemen riding towards them till they almost crashed into them. The boy they met pulled his pony to a halt and slid from the saddle. He looked up at Grace O'Malley's fierce face and grinned.

'Sorry. I'm in a hurry to get home.'

'What home would that be?' the woman asked.

'Howth castle,' the boy said. 'I'm Robyn, son of the Lord of Howth.'

Grace O'Malley turned her head slowly and looked at Mallen. The man in the leather jacket understood. He jumped down, grasped the boy and helped him back into his saddle. Then he took the reins and held them as he climbed back onto his own horse. He began to lead the boy down the hill.

The boy's servant on a grey donkey was confused. 'He's going the wrong way.' he cried.

Grace O'Malley leaned forward. From under her cloak a dagger appeared and it was at the throat of the startled servant before he could blink.

'Now, my little donkey,' she said, 'You can choose. Take a message to the Lord of Howth or have your throat cut.'

'Take a – take a – take a message,' the man babbled.

'Tell his lordship Grace O'Malley called for shelter and supper tonight. I was turned away from his door. There is an old Irish custom that says you always leave your door open and always have a spare place at your table for a weary traveller. His son will be on my ship. He can agree to lay that place at his table or I will drop his son into the Irish Sea. Understand?'

'Yes – yes.' The man dug his heels into the donkey and the animal trotted up the rocky road and disappeared into the gloom and mist.

When the mists had cleared and the morning sun sparkled on Dublin Bay a small boat rowed out to Grace O'Malley's ship. The Lord of Howth's servant was helped aboard and led before the captain. The man bowed his back and didn't dare look her in the eye. 'Captain O'Malley, I bring a message from the Lord of Howth.'

The woman nodded.

'His lordship says you are welcome to dine with him – at any time. There will always be a spare place set at the table in Howth Castle.'

That all happened four hundred years ago, they say. But if you go to Howth Castle today you will find there is an extra place at the table.

There now

Howth Castle is a family home. If you call and ask nicely they may let you look around … and keep a place at the tea table for you.

8. HOLYROOD PALACE
Edinburgh, Scotland

Mary, Queen of Scots, used Holyrood as her palace when she was in Scotland. She was married there ... twice ... so you probaly think it had happy memories for her, right? Wrong. She also watched a friend being murdered there.

David Rizzio - the sliced singer

David was a good singer and a nice lad. Some said he was an ugly little man, a bit of a big head who liked fancy clothes. But they all agreed he was a great singer.

I LOVE ME, YEAH, YEAH, YEAH

Mary liked his singing so much she gave him a job.

The queen started to trust him and turned to him for help. In 1565 Rizzo told her to marry Lord Darnley. The Scottish lords began to hate little David and plotted to kill him. Even Darnley was jealous.

It was 9 March, 1566. The queen was having her supper in the little room next to her bedroom at Holyrood. Suddenly

Darnley marched in, sat down beside Mary and started chatting to her.

Then Lord Ruthven appeared in the doorway, wearing full armour. He spoke…

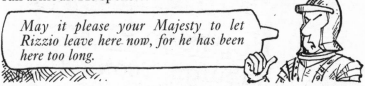

May it please your Majesty to let Rizzio leave here now, for he has been here too long.

But Mary was struck dumb. She rose to her feet in a panic. A terrified Rizzio hid behind her, clinging to her dress. He wailed…

Justice. Justice. Save my life, Madame, save me!

The queen couldn't save him because Andrew Kerr of Fawdonside held his pistol to her side, while George Douglas snatched Darnley's dagger from his belt and stabbed Rizzio.

Mary wrote in her diary that this first blow was struck over her shoulder.

The murderers dragged Rizzio from the room and hacked him to death. Darnley ordered that the body be flung down the staircase, and thrown across a casket where the porter's servant stripped him of his fine clothes.

THIS LOT'S GOING TO NEED A GOOD WASH AND A LOT OF PATCHES

Rizzio had been stabbed 56 times.

Mary wept. She asked over and over again what had happened to him. Hours later one of her ladies brought her the news. Rizzio was dead.

Mary dried her eyes and murmured ominously…

No more tears now, I will think upon revenge.

Darnley was later killed when his house blew up. Whodunnit? Who knows? But it didn't pay to mess with Mary.

Witch way to go

Mary's son, James, was worried by witchcraft. He was living at Holyrood when a witch, Agnes Sampson, was brought before him. She was accused of plotting to kill him. He had been sailing in the North Sea and they said she raised a storm to drown him. He said she did this by throwing bits of dead bodies tied to dead cats into the sea.

She was found guilty, taken to Castlehill in Edinburgh and burned.

Her naked ghost, known as Bald Agnes, is said to roam Holyrood Palace.

MOSTLY THE BATHROOMS

There now

The palace is owned by Queen Elizabeth II but you can visit if you pay her … or if she invites you.

9. GUNBY HALL
Lincolnshire, England

There have been a lot of killer women in the gruesome great houses of Britain ... Queen Mary I and her sister Elizabeth I sent hundreds to be executed.

But usually woeful women were the victims ... which may be why there are so many Grey Ladies and Green Ladies and White Ladies haunting those houses.

The Massingberd murder

🌿 Gunby Hall was built by Sir William Massingberd.

🌿 Sir William discovered that his daughter was about to run away with one of the servants, a coachman.

MY FATHER WON'T ALLOW US TO MARRY

THEN LET'S RUN AWAY TOGETHER

I'M NOT HAVING THAT

🌿 On the night the lovers intended to flee, Sir William hid and waited. He then shot the coachman dead.

❀ Sir William dragged the corpse through the gardens and threw it into the pond.

❀ Some reports say that Sir William was so angry he shot his daughter dead as well.

❀ The coachman's death put a curse on Gunby Hall. No male heir would ever go on to inherit the property. Oddly enough, none have.

❀ The ghost of the coachman can still be seen wandering by the pond, waiting for his love.

300 YEARS IS A LONG WAIT

Did you know?

Queen Victoria's favourite poet was the famous Alfred Tennyson. He visited Gunby Hall and wrote a poem about it. Alfred Tennyson was a miserable sort of child. He started writing poetry at a very young age and had written a 6000-line poem by the age of 12. But where did little Alf go for a nice quiet think? He spent a lot of time in the local churchyard, lying flat out amongst the gravestones.

He grew up to be famous and popular, invited to many parties. There he entertained the other guests by doing a party piece – pretending to be a person sitting on a toilet.

There now
Gunby Hall is open to the public.

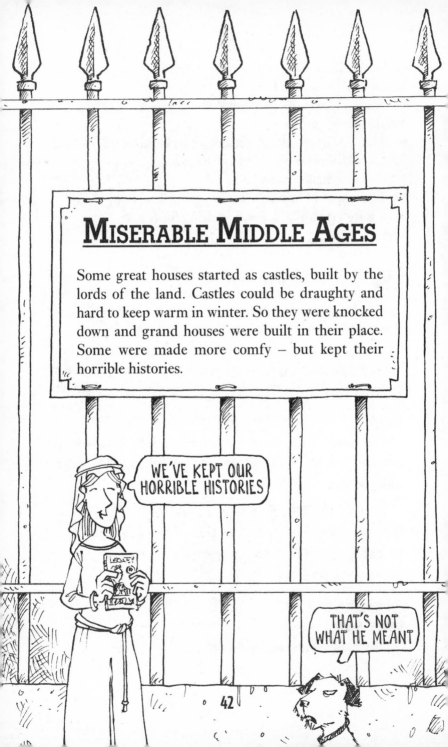

MISERABLE MIDDLE AGES

Some great houses started as castles, built by the lords of the land. Castles could be draughty and hard to keep warm in winter. So they were knocked down and grand houses were built in their place. Some were made more comfy – but kept their horrible histories.

WE'VE KEPT OUR HORRIBLE HISTORIES

THAT'S NOT WHAT HE MEANT

42

10. LUMLEY CASTLE
County Durham, England

Sir Ralph Lumley was made a Lord by King Richard II. He built a fine manor house at Lumley beside the River Wear. He was captured by the Scots at the Battle of Otterburn in 1388 but set free by 1389.

He came home and decided he'd better alter the house to make a castle in case those Scots marched back and battered him. Then, in 1399, Ralph's pal Richard II lost his throne to Henry IV.

The great stone walls and towers couldn't save Ralph when he marched south to attack new King Henry IV. That's treason. At Cirencester Ralph was beaten in battle and beheaded.

IT WAS A DAFT THING TO DO. I GUESS I JUST LOST MY HEAD

WELL, YOU WILL IN A MINUTE

That was not a good start to the life of Lumley.

Did you know?

Henry IV had the defeated King Richard II locked away in Pontefract Castle where he was probably starved to death in 1400.

Henry then faced a rebellion from Archbishop Scrope of York. Ruthless Henry sent Scrope to be executed. Scrope had to ride a bony old horse to his execution and sit facing backwards ... to make him look stupid.

A man called Tom Alman was given the job of beheading the bish. Tom had been a prisoner in York for 15 years and was told he could go free if he did the disgusting job.

It took him five chops to remove the head. Was he a botching bish butcher? No. Jesus had suffered five wounds when he was crucified, so the bishop requested to suffer five wounds too.

They also said a curse fell on Henry IV after killing Archbishop Scrope. He suffered a terrible skin disease, (maybe leprosy), and had terrible nightmares.

Terror tales

Over the years the windows at Lumley were made wider to let in light and it became more of a great house than a castle.

It also became one of the most haunted places in County Durham. Imagine you are lying in a Lumley bed, tossing and turning, then turning and tossing. It may be because of an old sausage you've eaten ... or it may be because of Lily.

🌸 Ralph Lumley had a wife called Lily. Lily did not like going to the Catholic church.

🌸 One day she was visited by two priests who tried to force her to worship as a Catholic.

🌸 When she refused they threw her down the castle well.

🌸 The priests told Ralph that Lily had gone off to become a nun. But her ghost floated up and haunts the castle to this day.

🌸 There is now Durham Cricket Ground across the river from the Castle. Cricketers often stay there. In 2005 the Australian cricket team stayed at Lumley. They were so scared of haunting happenings that some refused to sleep alone. Batty?
Cricketer Shane Watson said...

I didn't see anything but it was a very spooky sort of place and it definitely freaked me out. Will we stay there again? I hope not. I have bad memories. I didn't sleep for four nights.

There now

Lumley Castle is a hotel. You can stay in the haunted room ... if you dare.

NOT ME!

11. TREASURER'S HOUSE
York, England

The Normans invaded Britain in 1066 and built a massive cathedral in the North – York Minster. The man who looked after the money was the Treasurer and he had his own house, in the shadow of the cathedral. They called it the Treasurer's House – can't think why.

After 800 years it began to fall apart. You would too. Then along came a rich man called Frank Green and he repaired it and filled it with fine old furniture.

The incredible story

The Normans weren't the first to build on the spot. In 1953 an amazing story was told by a young man called Harry Martindale. Harry was a plumber sent to work on the pipes of the old house.

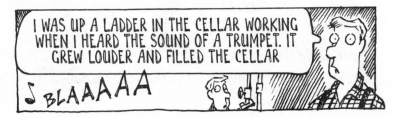

I WAS UP A LADDER IN THE CELLAR WORKING WHEN I HEARD THE SOUND OF A TRUMPET. IT GREW LOUDER AND FILLED THE CELLAR

♪ BLAAAAA

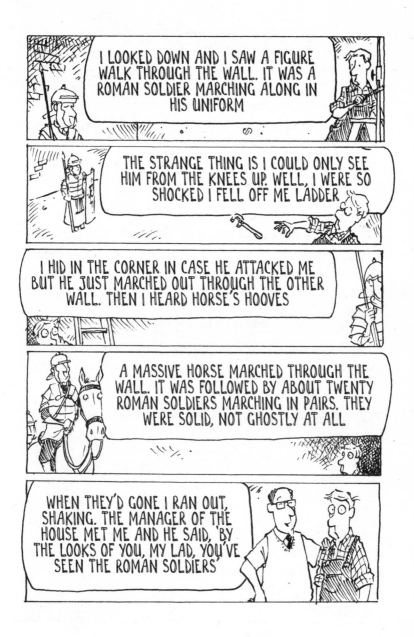

Harry gave up plumbing and became a policeman. But the ghostly Romans were seen again. Four years later the keeper of the house saw them three more times.

Why Roman soldiers? The floor was dug up years later and half a metre under the floor there was an ancient road. The house was built over one of the main Roman roads leading out of York to the North.

If a ghostly figure walked along the old Roman road they would have been seen from the knees upward ... just what Harry saw. Spooky?

Did you know?

Frank Green was a very fussy man. He had studs fixed to the floor in the rooms of Treasurer's House so the house maids knew exactly where his precious furniture should stand.

A kitchen maid told how Frank would inspect the kitchen. He emptied out any drawers he thought were untidy. A scary boss to have.

I'D RATHER SEE THE ROMANS

There now

The Treasurer's House – still filled with Frank Green's historic furniture – is open to the public.

12. DOLBADARN CASTLE
Gwynedd, Wales

Dolbadarn was one of three castles built by the Welsh prince Llywelyn the Great (1173–1240) during the early 1200s.

It was used as a great house for some years. Llywelyn the Great would have set out to hunt from Dolbadarn and travelled miles with his faithful hound, Gelert.

AH YES, THE TRAGIC TALE OF THE HERO HOUND. EVERY READER SHOULD KNOW IT

Gory for Gelert

In 1793 the owner of the Royal Goat Hotel came up with a great idea to attract visitors … the legend of how his village of Beddgelert got its name…

It all began with Prince Llywelyn the Great. He left Dolbadarn House to hunt in the mountains.
At the end of the day the hunters came to a valley and camped there.

The next morning the great warrior fed his baby son with goat's milk and left him in the tent while he went out hunting. He left the child in the care of his great hunting dog – Gelert.

While he was away a wolf came into the tent. And was just about to eat the baby. A tremendous fight took place (between the wolf and Gelert, not the baby and the wolf).

When Prince Llywelyn returned he found the tent in shreds and blood all over the hound. There was no sign of the baby. Llywelyn believed that Gelert had torn the child apart. Well, he would, wouldn't he? He took his war spear and thrust it through the hound.

No sooner had Gelert fallen to the ground than Llywelyn heard the baby crying under the torn tent. He pulled back the cover and there the child lay – without a mark on him – and the mangled corpse of the frightful wolf beside him.

Llywelyn was torn ... only not as torn as the wolf, of course. Torn between joy at his son's safety and grief at the death of his dog. He turned to the dog ... the dying animal licked his hand and then expired.

Llywelyn mourned his dog like a lost brother and buried him with a hero's funeral in a marvellous tomb.

There now

The castle fell into a ruin in the 1700s. Dolbadarn ruins are open to the public on certain dates.

There is a village called Beddgelert nearby. (It means the grave of Gelert.)

There is a pile of stones in the village that is said to be the hound's grave. The truth is the 'grave' was put there in 1793 by the landlord of the Goat Hotel in Beddgelert, David Pritchard. He wanted tourists to visit the village to see the grave ... and spend money in his hotel.

If the Gelert story was true it probably would have happened at Llywelyn's great house ... Dolbadarn Castle.

AH YES, THE TRAGIC TALE OF FACTS BEING MADE UP TO MAKE MONEY

13. TRETOWER COURT
Powys, Wales

Llywelyn the Great was one of the great Princes of Wales. But the English began to run the country and many Welsh people didn't like it. Their last great revolt was led by Owain Glyndŵr.

In 1400 some prophets in Wales said that the world would soon be coming to an end. Welsh peasants wanted to make the most of the time they had left. Their leader Owain Glyndŵr told them...

I have been chosen, by God, to release the Welsh from the slavery of our English enemies.

Gruesome Glyndŵr

Tretower was one of his targets. It was used as a stronghold by King Henry IV so Glyndŵr attacked it. He was held off by the English. Tretower was lucky. When Glyndŵr took Radnor Castle and 60 prisoners surrendered. Owain ordered...

EXECUTE THEM.
ALL OF THEM

Owain Glyndŵr could be pretty cruel in victory. It was said the castle keeper at Peterston–Super-Ely was beheaded after he surrendered.

Glyndŵr hung around at Tretower too long and an English army attacked him. They captured his flag and almost captured Glyndŵr himself.

The Welsh fled and the English followed … they followed into an ambush where a lot were cut down. And worse.

A writer told what the Welsh WOMEN got up to.

Now that's horrible history.

There now

Tretower Court is open to the public.

14. COTEHELE HOUSE
Cornwall, England

Some houses heard tales of terror told by troubadours, travelling singers, told around the fire. Tales like Robin Hood.

HANG ON. ROBIN HOOD WASN'T A TALE OF TERROR. HE ROBBED THE RICH AND GAVE TO THE POOR

NO. HE ROBBED THE RICH BECAUSE THE POOR HAD NOTHING WORTH PINCHING

THAT CLEVER GIRL HAS READ HER HORRIBLE HISTORIES BOOKS

Yes, Robin Hood and his gang of merry, murdering men made great songs and stories. Those old stories were far nastier than the Robin Hood tales we hear today.

LOOK AT LITTLE JOHN. IN THE OLD TALES NOT ONLY DOES HE HACK OFF THE HEAD OF A MONK, BUT HE KILLS THE MONK'S LITTLE PAGE-BOY IN COLD BLOOD JUST TO STOP HIM BEING A WITNESS

Cotehele House has a tale just as thrilling as Robin Hood's adventures and great escapes. Its true tale has been told by a poet.

The story is about Sir Richard Edgcumbe, the man who built Cotehele in 1485 and also built a chapel by the river. The history books say he was at war with rotten King Richard III and Richard's men hunted him down in the woods near Cotehele. He came out of the woods and faced the deep river.

With that river in front of him he was trapped. His enemy was coming through the trees behind him with their hunting hounds on his heels.

Yes. Hounds on his heels. A minstrel wrote a v-e-r-y long poem about what happened next. Too long. So we hired the Horrible Histories minstrel to write a shorter poem. (We paid him 10p for his work. Some would say it was 9p too much.)

1
Sir Richard through the woodland fled,
The king's men cried, 'We want him dead.
He hates the king, he is a sinner.
We'll serve him up for our hounds' dinner.'
('Oh woof,' the hounds thought.)

2
Through the woodland, hedge and ditch,
Ran the sweating old Sir Rich.
Reached a cliff and down below
He saw the raging river flow.
('And I can't even swim.')
3
'I'm dead as a doornail,' thought Sir Dick,
Until he started thinking quick.
He stuffed a stone into his hat,
Then threw it in the river. Splat.
(Hat floated. Dick hid in the trees.)
4
The hunters heard the splash and saw
The hat float off so far from shore.
'He's jumped and killed himself,' they said.
'Let's all go home. Sir Richard's dead.'
(Oh no he isn't.)
5
He lived to fight another day
And Richard Three he helped to slay.
He built beside the river banks
A church to give to God his thanks.
(But he never got his hat back.)

There now

The house is open to visitors – it has no electric lighting inside, so watch your step.

The Chapel-in-the-Wood, on the riverside path between the house and the river, is also open to visitors.

CURSED AND GONE

Some gruesome great houses seem to curse the owners. Everyone is happy when these cursed houses are gone and have taken their bad luck with them.

Here are a few that you can't see today…

15. WITLEY PARK
Surrey, England

❀ Witley Park was as old as the Normans. A rich man called Whitaker Wright bought the land in 1890 and built a grand house there.

❀ He flattened hills, dug lakes and under one of the lakes he even built an underwater ballroom where he could entertain guests, play billiards and dance.

❀ He lost all his money and in 1904 he was sent to jail for cheating people out of their money.

❀ He didn't want to go to jail so he took a pill filled with the poison cyanide and died horribly.

❀ The house was sold to Lord Pirrie ... the man who built the cursed ship *Titanic*.

❀ After Lord Pirrie died Witley Park slowly fell into ruin and then a mystery fire finished it off in 1952.

16. MILNER FIELD
West Yorkshire, England

🌸 Milner Field house was built in 1869 by Titus Salt Jr whose father made a fortune in the wool business. Kind Titus Salt Senior built the large village of Saltaire for his workers.

🌸 Salt Senior died in 1876 and Titus Junior took over the wool business but it began to fail and Junior, who had a weak heart, died in 1887. The house was sold to man named James Roberts, who had even more bad luck.

🌸 One of his sons died from pneumonia, another drowned on holiday in Ireland, another died of a 'nervous illness' then his fourth son was badly wounded in World War I, and was never able to work.

🌸 Roberts's daughter, Alice, ran away to marry Norman Rutherford, a man Roberts disapproved of. But then she fell for another man – her husband's friend – so her husband shot his mate dead. Rutherford spent 10 years in Broadmoor prison and lost his fortune.

🌸 The house's final owner met a gruesome end when he hiccupped himself to death. (No, honestly.) The house was knocked down in the 1950s.

HIC!

17. PETERWELL
Ceredigion, Wales

🌸 The curse at Peterwell started in the 1600s. There was a house called Maesyfelin where Ellen Lloyd lived. She told her brothers that she planned to marry her lover, Samuel Prichard.

🌸 The brothers were furious. When their father died they'd have to share the wealth between the four brothers – but if Ellen married, then they would have to share it with him too. They wanted to get rid of him. So they tied Sam to the back of his horse and let it drag him all the way home to Llandovery. It killed him of course. They cut the body from the back of the horse and threw it in the River Tywi.

HE WAS A DEAD WEIGHT

🌸 Samuel's dad, a vicar, placed a curse on the Lloyd family AND on the house at Maesyfelin. It worked. First Ellen went mad with misery and died. Then the eldest son murdered his

three brothers; he then hanged himself and the house burned to the ground. Of course, this tale is probably untrue. It is just a story told by the folk of Lampeter to explain the ruin.

🌹 Or was it untrue? A hundred years later Herbert Lloyd, from the same family, used the stones from the ruined house to build a new house, Peterwell. And the curse went with the stones.

🌹 One of Herbert Lloyd's most evil acts was to blame an old farmer for stealing a sheep. The old man was hanged and horrible Herbert took his land. But Herbert owed a fortune in money so he shot himself.

🌹 Herbert Lloyd's body was taken back to Peterwell and laid in the coffin ready for burial. The lawyers pinned a note to the coffin saying he couldn't be buried till everyone had been paid what he owed them. The coffin was a guarded for weeks to make sure he wasn't buried. It was summer and the body would go mouldy pretty quickly. Very mouldy – very smelly. In the end the servants at Peterwell got the guards drunk. They stole the coffin and buried the cursed corpse.

18. CLUMBER HOUSE
Nottinghamshire, England

🌸 Clumber was a monastery during the days of the Normans. Then along came Henry VIII and closed it down. It was a bad-habit day.

🌸 In the early 1700s the land became a great place to hunt harmless little animals like deer. Clumber House was built from the stones of the old monastery around 1760.

🌸 The rich owners filled it like a treasure chest full of paintings and books. But those old monks, who led a simple life, must have brought a curse on the place.

🌸 In 1789 a fire raged through the house and destroyed many of the great paintings. The house could be repainted – the paintings couldn't.

🌸 The house was rebuilt. But in 1912 another fire swept through it and this time it was left to crumble. It was demolished in 1938. BUT there was a strange story that Clumber House wasn't actually destroyed. The locals said a rich American took it away, stone by stone, and built it up again … in Arizona, USA.

TERRIFYING TUDORS

A lot of great houses were built in the Tudor age. King Henry VIII closed down the monasteries and sold off the land to the rich.

They didn't build castles because cannons had been invented. Cannons could blow down castle walls so castles weren't used much any more. But the Tudors *did* build great houses ... they often used the stones from the monasteries.

King Henry VIII was the most terrifying of the Tudors. He is remembered for the awful way he treated his wives.

19. BLICKLING HALL
Norfolk, England

Blickling Hall was the family home of Henry VIII's second wife, Anne Boleyn. Her enemies said Anne poisoned Henry's first wife, Catherine. That's nonsense, but it was true that Anne was happy to see Henry's opponents go for the chop. One of them was an old friend of Henry's, Sir Thomas More. As he went to the scaffold he said:

Anne Boleyn might strike our heads off like footballs, but it won't be long before her head will dance the same dance.

I'VE NEVER SEEN A DANCING FOOTBALL

Tom was right. Henry grew fed up with Anne when she failed to give him a son. He had her executed for flirting with other men.

What the school history books don't tell you is how kind old Henry was when it came to Anne's execution. He didn't want any of that hacking about and sawing at necks. He sent for a real expert. A swordsman.

Anne Boleyn didn't have to lay her neck on a block. She walked onto the scaffold, said a few words of farewell and was blindfolded. The swordsman didn't want her turned towards him so he said...

Clean off, first time. (Unlike a French swordsman who took 29 swings of the sword to execute the Count of Chalais in 1626.)

Hundreds of years later there were ghost stories of Anne wandering round the Tower of London with her head tucked underneath her arm.

In the 1930s there was a popular song about the ghost...

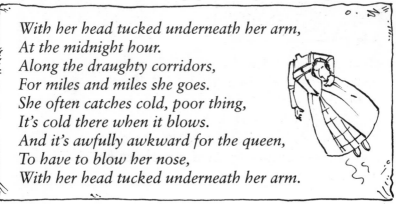

With her head tucked underneath her arm,
At the midnight hour.
Along the draughty corridors,
For miles and miles she goes.
She often catches cold, poor thing,
It's cold there when it blows.
And it's awfully awkward for the queen,
To have to blow her nose,
With her head tucked underneath her arm.

But there were different ghost stories told at the time of the execution. They said…

🐾 Candles around the tomb of Catherine of Aragon, Anne's enemy, burst into flame the day before the execution. As the blow fell on Anne's neck the next day the candles went out just as mysteriously.

🐾 As Anne died people reported seeing hares running across the fields – a hare was the sign of a witch and Anne was suspected of witchcraft. Every year on 19 May, the day of her death, hares were seen. Perhaps they still are. That's Anne Boleyn all over – hare today and gone tomorrow.

🐾 At Blickling Hall Anne's ghost has been seen racing at high speed in a ghostly carriage pulled by headless horses and a headless horseman. The driver is said to be her father, Thomas Boleyn. The story says that he must drive this carriage with his headless daughter in the back for a thousand years.

✤ Sir Henry Hobart lived at Blickling Hall. In 1698 he argued with his neighbour, Oliver Le Neve. Le Neve called Hobart a 'coward'. Sir Henry flew into a rage...

They fought. Oliver Le Neve was a poor fighter ... but he wounded Sir Henry. The next day the owner of Blickling Hall died in his bedroom in the western tower. Creepy groaning noises have been heard in that room ever since and dogs refuse to enter it.

There now

The hall where Anne lived was knocked down to make way for the mansion you see today. But on 19 May each year the phantom carriage can still be heard.

20. HATFIELD HOUSE
Hertfordshire, England

Hatfield house started life as Hatfield Palace. In 1558 Anne Boleyn's daughter, Elizabeth I, was sitting reading in the garden of the palace, the place where she had grown up. They say she was reading a Bible. (It was definitely not a Horrible Histories book.) Then some important news came...

YOUR SISTER, MARY TUDOR, IS DEAD. YOU ARE NOW THE NEW QUEEN OF ENGLAND

OOOOH. GOODY

Elizabeth was thrilled to hear her half-sister Mary was dead. A lot of people were pleased ... mind you, the hundreds of people Mary had burned alive were too dead to be pleased.

Did you know?

When Mary Tudor became queen she had some of her enemies executed. The Duke of Northumberland was one of the first to go. He was hanged by the neck till he was half dead, split open and made to watch his guts burn. He was then beheaded and cut into four pieces. Ouch.

Mary added an extra punishment…

In 1603 King James I came to the throne in England and Ireland. His chief minister, Robert Cecil, moved into Hatfield Palace. What did Robert do with it? In 1607 he knocked most of the palace down to build Hatfield House. But some of the old palace still remained. Robert Cecil let it stand … as stables.

Robert Cecil's new house was almost finished but he wasn't there to have a house-warming party. He did a careless thing. He died.

In 1835 the west wing of Hatfield House burned down. Lady Emily Mary Hill was in it at the time. She was 85 years old and couldn't get out. She didn't live to be 86. Some say she was wearing feathers in her hair and as she leaned forward the feathers caught a candle flame and started the fatal fire.

Then the wind changed and rain fell so the chapel at Hatfield House was saved from the frightful flames – God must have been smiling on it. But not on poor Lady Emily.

There now

Today you can see little gunshot marks in the Old Palace's roof beams – some say sparrows flew in during the time it was a stables and were shot.

It is open to the public on certain days each year.

21. GLAMIS CASTLE
Angus, Scotland

It's said that Anne Boleyn had six fingers on one hand, which her enemies said proved she was a witch ... which she wasn't, of course.

In England, witches were hanged. But in Scotland witches were burned … a slow and horrible way to die.

NEARLY AS HORRIBLE AS SCOTLAND'S OTHER FAVOURITE ... A CHOCOLATE BAR DIPPED IN BATTER AND DEEP FRIED IN BOILING FAT

HELP!

Janet Douglas was Lady of Glamis in 1537 and hated King James V of Scotland so much she tried to poison him. At least that's what James said. It was probably just an excuse to get rid of her.

Janet of Glamis Castle was taken to Edinburgh Castle and put on trial. Her servants and her family were tortured till they said the murder plot was true.

Of course she was found guilty and taken out into the yard of Edinburgh Castle. Her husband didn't try to rescue her – he ran off to England. Janet was tied to a stake and burned to death. Her son, John, had already been stretched on the rack to force him to talk. He was made to watch Mum's execution.

So was Janet really wicked? People said she'd already poisoned her first husband and got away with it. But that probably wasn't true, either.

James V took over Glamis Castle but Janet's ghost got there first. She is the Grey Lady that still haunts the clock tower of the castle.

Deadly doors

Glamis Castle was a good place to die.

🌸 King Malcolm 'The Destroyer' was murdered there.

🌸 There is a 'Room of Skulls' where the Ogilvie family tried to shelter from the Lindsays and were walled up and left to die of starvation.

🌸 The 'Monster of Glamis' is said to have lived there. A disfigured child who was locked away and then buried in the walls when he died.

🌸 Earl Beardie of Glamis was a wicked man who liked card games. He tried playing instead of praying on a Sunday. A stranger then appeared at the castle and joined Lord Beardie in a game of cards. But the stranger was the devil who took Beardie's soul – the lord had to play cards in hell forever more.

🌸 Glamis even has its own water monster like the one in Loch Ness. It lives in Loch Calder near the castle. It may not be Nessie...

There now

Glamis is still there and open to visitors on certain days each year.

22. LEDSTON HALL
West Yorkshire, England

Henry VIII had closed down the monasteries like Pontefract Priory. Great houses had been built in their places. Houses like Ledston Hall.

Ledston has a gruesome tale to tell. It's another witch story.

In Tudor times the poor people could not afford a doctor. When someone was sick they went to the 'wise man' or the 'wise woman' of the village. The trouble came when one of their cures went wrong. The villagers stopped calling them 'wise' and called them 'witch'. There could be terrible punishments for anyone called a witch.

In Ledston the 'wise woman' was called Mary Pannell. Most of the time she worked as a servant in the great hall but helped the poor in Ledston village when they fell ill.

Everyone was happy until…

THE LORD OF LEDSTON HALL HAD A SON

OUR SON HAS STOMACH PAINS

MARY PANNELL WILL HAVE A CURE

That story could be true. There's just one thing wrong with it. In Scotland witches were burned to death. But, as you know, in England they were hanged.

Is Mary's sad story true? It's a history mystery.

There now

Ledston Hall is still there. The hill where Mary was 'burned' is known as Mary Pannell Hill.

23. PLAS MAWR
Conwy County, Wales

In the days of the Tudors Sir Robert Wynn built a 'Great Hall' –
or 'Plas Mawr' in Welsh. He had a lovely wife, Dorothy, and a
fine son.

And did they all live happy ever after? Of course they didn't.

THIS IS A HORRIBLE HISTORIES
BOOK SO WHAT DO YOU EXPECT?

The legend goes that Sir Robert went off to fight over
seas. He went to fight and kill for Queen Elizabeth. Dorothy
and son waited for a letter. Then it arrived. Had he died in
the war with a sword up his nose? No. He was on the way
home.

DADDY'S
COMING
HOME

WHO?

So Dorothy and son toddled up the steep stone steps every day to look out for him from the top of the tower. At the end of a boring day they plodded back down. Day after day. Then day after another day. They sat in the icy winds and watched and waited. Maybe the cold wind froze Lady Wynn's legs? We'll never know. What we do know is she stumbled and fell, wig over slippers, all the way to the bottom. And she took young Master Wynn with her.

OUCH

The servants found them badly injured at the bottom of the steps. They took them to the lantern room and sent for the doctor. He was away. Oh, no. So they let his young assistant, Doctor Dic, look at them. He panicked.

THEIR SKULLS ARE SMASHED, SHATTERED, CRACKED AND CRUSHED. LOOK THEIR BRAINS ARE LEAKING OUT

THEY'RE A BIT POORLY THEN?

SIR ROBERT IS COMING DOWN THE ROAD. HE'LL BE FURIOUS

Doctor Dic tried to make a run for it, but the servants locked him in the lantern room with the bodies. Then they welcomed Sir Robert.

Sir Robert was furious. He swore he'd kill young Doctor Dic. The doc heard his lord rage and searched for somewhere to hide. But there wasn't anywhere to go.

Sir Robert drew his dagger, burst into the room and found Dr Dic ... nowhere. The doctor had vanished from a locked room. In fact, he was never ever seen again. (Local people say he may have crawled up the chimney.)

Sir Robert was so upset he stabbed someone else in the neck till they bled to death. Who did he stab? Himself. Yes, raging Robert killed himself.

But the servants probably lived happy ever after.

There now

Plas Mawr is still there and open to the public. Just watch your step. Listen for the footsteps in the lantern room in the dead of night. Sir Robert Wynn is still looking for Doctor Dic.

24. CHATSWORTH HOUSE
Derbyshire, England

Elizabeth Talbot – known as Bess of Hardwick – was a Derbyshire woman. She was probably the richest and most powerful woman in Tudor England. How did she do it? She married four times and was a very clever person. She made her fortunes from coal mining and glass factories.

🌸 Her first husband died on Christmas Eve 1544. She was 17 and he was just 14.

WELL THAT'S RUINED MY CHRISTMAS

IT HASN'T DONE MUCH FOR MINE EITHER, MATE

🌸 Bess married William Cavendish in 1547. He made his fortune from the monasteries Henry VIII had closed down. They had eight children in the next ten years. He built Chatsworth House for Bess then popped his clogs, hopped the twig and kicked the bucket.

❀ Her third husband, William, was Elizabeth I's Captain of the Guard. He died in 1565 … maybe poisoned by his own brother. He left her a fortune and she became Lady of the Bedchamber to Queen Elizabeth.

❀ She married George Talbot who had been married before and had seven children of his own. Two of his children married two of hers at the same wedding.

❀ Elizabeth I's cousin, Mary, Queen of Scots, was unpopular in Scotland – she had a husband murdered and other little things like that. She ran off to England and begged Elizabeth to protect her. Elizabeth locked her away at Chatsworth

House and Bess was one of her jailers. Bess and Mary did a lot of sewing together. Mary was beheaded in 1587.

THAT'S SEW, SEW SAD

🌸 Bess married off one of her daughters to Mary, Queen of Scots's brother-in-law. Queen Elizabeth was furious and ordered Bess to appear in London and answer questions. Bess just refused to go and stayed in the North until Elizabeth calmed down.

SHE'S SO, SO MAD

🌸 Bess's granddaughter, Arbella, was also a relative of Mary, Queen of Scots, so she could claim the throne when Elizabeth I died in 1603. Arbella wanted to run away to marry her love. What did Bess of Hardwick do when she heard of the plot? Locked Arbella away to stop her. Arbella never forgave Granny Bess.

There now

Chatsworth House is open to the public most of the year – and the sewing that Mary and Bess did together can be seen at Oxburgh Hall in Norfolk.

Did you know?

Oxburgh Hall in Norfolk is famous for having a 'priest hole'. That was a secret hiding place where Catholics could hide when their Protestant enemies hunted them down.

The Bedingfield family lived there and held Catholic church services. Priests would hide in the priest hole under a trapdoor in the floor.

How did they tell people a Catholic service was being held? A secret signal was used – the washing was left out.

Bess of Hardwick croaked in 1608. Elizabeth I had died in 1603 and the Stuart family came to the throne.

25. BUCKLAND ABBEY
Devon, England

The Spanish didn't like Elizabeth I or her sailors. Sailors like Francis Drake who sailed around the world. He set off in November 1577 with a little fleet. Only the *Pelican* made the trip through the storms at the southern tip of South America. He changed her name to *Golden Hind*.

On the way he raided the Spanish port of Valparaiso using a trick – he pretended to be friendly, captured Spanish sailors and made them hand over their treasure.

At the end of his voyage he returned home in September 1580 to be made a knight – Sir Francis Drake. But his pirating had upset the Spanish, so they sent a great armada of ships to invade England in 1588. The English fleet – with a little help from some storms – defeated the Spanish.

The Spanish thought Drake was a devil and wrote poems about him. They said he was not 'Drake' but 'Draco' … a dragon. Poet Lope wrote about Draco Drake…

His eyes of blue shone like the light of dawn;
His fiery breath lit up the heavens on high;
His nostrils poured out black and smoking clouds;
His mouth sent tongues of flame into the sky.

TOO MUCH CHILLI

Drake used his fortune to buy Buckland Abbey in Devon. There are some famous stories about Drake…

Drake's tale 1

SIR FRANCIS WAS PLAYING BOWLS WHEN THE ARMADA WAS SIGHTED. HE SAID HE'D FINISH HIS GAME OF BOWLS FIRST, 'THERE'S TIME FOR THAT AND TIME TO BEAT THE SPANIARDS AFTER'

Did you know?

Amazingly, it's said that the Spanish Armada gunners didn't score a single hit.

MISSED ME

Drake's tale 2

There was an old drum that Drake took with him on his journey around the world. As Drake lay dying he ordered that the drum be sent back to Buckland Abbey.

IN TIMES OF TROUBLE IT SHOULD BE BEATEN. THAT WILL RECALL ME FROM HEAVEN TO RESCUE MY COUNTRY

Some people say the drum sounds itself as a warning whenever England is in danger. Many people have claimed they heard the drum in wartime.

Drake's Drum was last heard during World War II when German bombers began the Battle of Britain.

But Drake didn't show up in *Golden Hind* and shoot them down.

There now

Buckland Abbey is open to the public ... and visitors think they can see Drake's Drum. They can't. Drake's Drum is locked away in a cool, dry store hundreds of miles away where it won't rot. The drum you can see at Buckland is a copy.

WHY IS A BROKEN DRUM THE BEST TOY IN THE WORLD?

I DON'T KNOW. WHY?

BECAUSE YOU CAN'T BEAT IT!

SLIMY STUARTS

James I was the first of the Stuart kings to rule in England (but the sixth Scottish king called James). In England Guy Fawkes tried to blow him up in the Gunpowder Plot.

26. COUGHTON COURT
Warwickshire, England

Coughton Court was one of the Catholic houses that had a 'priest hole' to hide their friends when Elizabeth I's army came to arrest them.

The Throckmorton plot

The Catholic Throckmortons were fed up with the torturing Tudor queen so they plotted to kill her.

In 1583 there was the Throckmorton Plot. The chief plotter was called Throckmorton ... you probably guessed that. Francis of that name was first cousin to Elizabeth's lady-in-waiting. Always handy to have friends in high places.

The plot was simple.

🌸 Assassinate Elizabeth

🌸 Join with French invaders led by Henry I Duke of Guise

🌸 Stir up a revolt of English Catholics backed by the Pope and Spanish gold

🌸 Place Mary, Queen of Scots on the English throne

Elizabeth's spymaster, Sir Francis Walsingham, heard of the plot and found proof in Throckmorton's house. Throckmorton said…

IT WASN'T ME!

Walsingham's torturers set to work on him. Throckmorton said…

OH, ALL RIGHT. IT WAS ME

He was executed.

The powder plot

Queen Liz died in 1603 and James took the throne. Again, the Catholics wanted a Catholic on the throne and plotted to assassinate James (and a few hundred friends) in the Gunpowder Plot of 1605. Gunpowder would explode under the Houses of Parliament when James went there on 5 November.

The plotters rented Coughton Court for a meeting place. It was Guy Fawkes who was left to light the fuse on the gunpowder, then escape. But on 4 November, Guy was caught and tortured.

One of the other plotters, Bates, rushed to Coughton Court and asked the Catholic priests there for help in raising an army. The reply was surprising. The leader of the priests, Father Garnet, said…

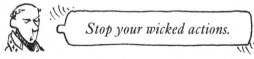

Stop your wicked actions.

The priests ran off to hide. They were caught, and then imprisoned in London.

There now

The house is open to the public throughout the year.

27. HOLBECHE HOUSE
West Midlands, England

When the powder plotters heard about the arrest of Guy Fawkes, they fled from Coughton and their homes and took shelter in Holbeche House.

They had taken weapons and gunpowder from Hewell Grange on 7 November 1605. Stephen Lyttleton rode to his house at Holbeche with Sir Everard Digby, John and Robert Winter and the leader of the plot, Robert Catesby.

They crossed the River Stour and decided to put up a last fight at Holbeche. The Sheriff's men were close behind and quickly surrounded the house.

The plotters had ridden their horses straight into the main hall of the large house, where they discovered that their gunpowder had become wet during the river crossing.

The servants used furniture from the room to build a roaring fire, around which they placed the damp powder.

SPREAD IT OUT IN FRONT OF THE FIRE TO DRY

ISN'T THAT DANGEROUS?

NAH. EVERYBODY KNOWS GUNPOWDER ONLY EXPLODES WHEN IT'S PRESSED DOWN HARD IN A TIGHT SPACE

He was right. Sort of. Gunpowder may not explode … but it does burn fiercely. A spark from the fire started a terrible blaze. Several of the plotters were badly burned and one was blinded. (Nay, don't know what happened to the horses.)

At about noon the next day, 8 November 1605, 200 men from the Sheriff's forces attacked. Most of the plotters were either killed or wounded in the fight.

Those who were captured alive were taken to London, where they were tortured and executed.

Did you know?

Two of the plotters, Thomas Percy and leader Robert Catesby, stood back-to-back to fight off the Sheriff's men. One bullet killed them both.

Catesby and Percy may have escaped the torture and execution, but their bodies were dug up. Their dead heads were cut off and stuck on spikes outside the House of Lords in London. The living plotters were executed and their heads joined Catesby's and Percy's.

There now

Gideon Grove was just a stable lad at Holbeche. He ran from the blaze but was shot by mistake. His ghost can be seen there. It's known as 'The Headless Horseman of Holbeche'. The house is now a nursing home. Some walls have holes from muskets used in the attack on the house in 1605.

28. MARPLE HALL
Greater Manchester, England

James's son, Charles I, caused a lot of trouble when he said he could rule England and Scotland with no help from Parliament. So Parliament's soldiers (the Roundheads) went to war with the king's soldiers (the Cavaliers). The battles are known as the English Civil War.

You had to choose which side you were on. The English Civil War caused a lot of misery … and murder.

The story of Esther and her boyfriend Legh is like the tale of Romeo and Juliet. Esther lived with her father, a Roundhead, at Marple Hall and Legh, a Cavalier, came from the nearby Lyme Hall.

Legh was never seen alive again. Esther died from a broken heart a year later. Her ghost walks the corridors of Marple Hall. She had company – NOT young Legh, but King Charles I himself.

Why does King Charles wander round an enemy house? Horrible Henry Bradshaw had a brother, John, who signed the order that sent Charles to his execution. Does chopped Charlie seek revenge?

There now

Marple Hall was left to fall into ruin. It was knocked down in the 1950s. Only a stone doorstep in a field remains. It's as dead as young Legh.

The name Marple is from the words 'Mere pool' – a swampy pond. There's a Marple Hall School there now. That's life. Pool today, school tomorrow.

Charles got the chop in 1649 and the Roundheads won the war.

29. CLAYDON HOUSE
Buckinghamshire, England

Another victim of the English Civil War was Edmund Verney. Edmund lived at Claydon House and became a high-class servant to King Charles I.

Ed went to Spain with his king when Charles went there to chat up the Princess Maria. Of course, the English were Protestants and the Spanish were Catholics.

One Englishman fell ill and was dying so a Catholic priest came to pray for him. Ed (a Protestant) was furious.

What did angry Ed do?

a) Burst into tears
b) Burst a balloon full of water over the priest
c) Burst the priest's nose with a punch in the face

Answer (c)

Edmund was NOT popular with the Spanish after clobbering the cleric.

The disappearance of Edmund

When Charles fought against Parliament in the English Civil War Edmund Verney fought by the king's side. Ed's job was to carry the banner – the flag that the Cavaliers followed into battle.

His eldest son fought for the other side, the Roundheads. Would you do that to your dad?

Edmund fought at the Battle of Edgehill on 23 October 1642. Edmund was never seen again and his body was never found on the battlefield.

BUT ... the banner was found. And wrapped around the pole was Edmund's hand.

HAND OVER THE BANNER!

HA HA

His ghost is said to haunt Claydon House.

There now

There is a small museum at Claydon to remember Florence Nightingale, the famous nurse. Florence's sister married one of the Verney family. She was a hundred years too late to nurse Edmund's hand ... even if they could have found the rest of his body.

The Verney family still live in part of the house and the rest is open to the public.

30. LISSAN HOUSE
County Tyrone, Northern Ireland

Thomas Staples from Bristol built the first family home at Lissan, in Northern Ireland, around 1620. Why? Because there was precious iron on the land and mighty oak trees that could be cut down to smelt the iron in the furnaces.

But the Staples family weren't the only ones who wanted that iron. The Catholic Irish wanted the Protestant English rulers to give them more freedom. The Irish rebelled.

Where would they get iron for their weapons? Places like Lissan of course. Lady Staples told a terrible tale…

IN 1641 THE REBELS LOCKED ME AND MY FOUR CHILDREN AWAY IN THE CASTLE AT CASTLECAULFIELD. THEY HELD US FOR TWO YEARS. POOR KIDS

THEY USED OUR LISSAN HOUSE SERVANTS TO MAKE THEIR WEAPONS AND TREATED THEM LIKE SLAVES

IF ANYONE REFUSED TO HELP, THE REBELS MURDERED WHOLE FAMILIES – AND THEY DID IT OUTSIDE THE WINDOW OF MY PRISON

LIFE WAS SO HARD IN THE SLAVE GANGS OUR SERVANTS BEGGED THE REBELS TO KILL THEM AND STOP THE MISERY

OUR HOUSE AT LISSAN WASN'T DAMAGED BECAUSE OUR IRON WORKS WERE TOO PRECIOUS

BUT WHEN WE GOT HOME WE FOUND THE TOWN NEXT DOOR, COOKSTOWN, WAS DESTROYED

Around 12,000 Protestants may have died in the rebellion – most of them dying of cold or disease after being thrown out of their homes in the bitter winter. The horrors went on...

Dreadful diary of the Irish Rebellion

🌸 **1641** There were 100 Protestants thrown off a bridge at Portadown (County Armagh) to drown.

🌸 **1642** The Protestants fought back. It's said that as many as 3000 Catholics were thrown to their deaths over the cliffs at Islandmagee.

🌸 **1649** Chief Roundhead, Oliver Cromwell arrived from England. He calls Ireland:

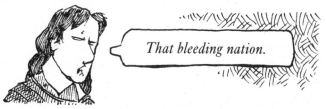

That bleeding nation.

He doesn't mess about with revolting Catholics, he has them killed. He stays just nine months yet his horrors will be remembered in Ireland for hundreds of years.

Did you know?

After the rebellion was crushed, Catholic children were banned from going to school ... some young people today may think that's a good thing.

There now

Lissan House is open to the public.

31. CROM CASTLE
Fermanagh, Northern Ireland

The Irish Rebellion was cruel. There was worse to come. In 1688 King James II was thrown off the throne for being a Catholic. He went to Ireland. He hoped an army of Irish Catholics would help him snatch back the throne of England and Scotland.

Old books tell the tale of Viscount Galmoy. He was a brutal man.

> **V**iscount Galmoy attacked Crom Castle with a tin gun that was made to look like a great iron cannon. When he tried to fire it the tin gun blew up. Galmoy was driven back. He swore revenge.
>
> As he rode away in a rage he came across two young friends driving cattle. They were Mr Dixie and Mr Charlton, with a few friends helping.
>
> 'You are a troop of soldiers,' Galmoy said. 'We arrest you and you shall hang.'
>
> 'No,' Mr Dixie said. 'These are my father's cattle and we are taking them to him.'

'No, you are soldiers and traitors. You must hang,' said Galmoy. Mr Dixie had just come from college in Dublin and was no soldier. But Viscount Galmoy's men took him back to their fortress at Belturbet anyway. There they hanged him from the town gates.

The rope snapped and he fell to the ground alive. He asked him, 'Will you change sides?'

Mr Dixie refused so they hanged him a second time with his friend Mr Charlton. Then they cut off their heads and played football with them through the streets, fixing the heads to the door of the Market House when they were done.

All this because Viscount Galmoy was angry about failing to capture Crom Castle with his tiny tin cannon.

SO WERE THE VICTIMS CATHOLICS OR PROTESTANTS?

THEY WERE HUMAN BEINGS

Galmoy went on slaughtering his enemies. To the north of Crom he captured a father and son. He forced the son to hang his father then carry his head around the town with a sign saying, 'This is a traitor'. Then he hanged the son.

There now

You can stay in part of Crom Castle. The old Crom Castle – the bit attacked with a tin gun – is a ruin, open to the public at certain times each year.

32. PREHEN HOUSE
County Londonderry, Northern Ireland

Half-hanged McNaughton

Hanging someone twice was not unusual in the days of executions. Another man to be hanged twice was John McNaughton. He was given the name 'Half-hanged McNaughton' which is odd. He should have been named: 'Half-hanged-the-first-time-but-twice-hanged-in-the-end-McNaughton'.

FIRST THEY HANGED ME A LITTLE, THEN THEY HANGED ME A LOT

It was HIS fault he was hanged twice though.

The story started at Prehen House where the Knox family lived. John went there to visit his friend, Andrew Knox. Then John fell in love with Knox's daughter, Anne. He even said he had married her in secret. Anne was 15 years old.

Anne's father, Andrew Knox, said he was taking her away from Prehen to live in Dublin and get away from John. That's when John came up with a daring plot to kidnap her. A newspaper of the time may have reported it like this.

FREE TICKETS TO ANY PRIME TIME HANGING OF YOUR CHOICE

9 December 1761

The DERRY DAILY NEWS

Don't be armless - win a pistol in our GET-A-GUN competition

MURDERER McNAUGHTON CAUGHT

John McNaughton was a tax-collector in Coleraine till he started spending the taxes on gambling. His only friend was Andrew Knox of Prehen House. How did McNaughton repay his friend? He tried to kidnap Knox's daughter, Anne.

On 10 November McNaughton and his gang hid near Burndennett Bridge. When the Knox coach came along, they rode out with pistols. A gun fight followed with the Knox guards. In the fight one of McNaughton's bullets struck poor Anne and she died.

McNaughton was wounded but escaped for a while. He was later arrested, hiding in a hay barn.

Andrew Knox wept for his daughter and said, 'He deserves it. He was a penniless gambler when I helped him and invited him to Prehen House. He didn't want Anne for love. He wanted her for her fortune.'

McNaughton's trial took place yesterday, and he was sentenced to be hanged. The hanging will be next Tuesday in an open field at Strabane so all the people of Derry can watch.

On 15 December 1761 thousands of people DID come to watch. McNaughton said…

The rope was placed around his neck. He hurled himself off the platform so his end would come quickly. But he tried too hard. The rope snapped and the crowd shouted for him to…

He was hanged again … the rope did not break a second time. McNaughton lost his life, but his name lives on in a legend that makes him sound like a hero. The truth is he was desperate for Anne's £5,000 fortune and stalked her for two years till he had the chance to attack.

There now

In one of the fields near Prehen House, there is a tree known as the 'Post Office Tree'. That was the tree where McNaughton and Anne Knox secretly left love letters.

Over the years, visitors to Prehen House have spotted the figure of a man hanging around in the grounds, and a young woman in 1760s costume roaming close by.

Prehen is open to the public. So is Strabane graveyard, where McNaughton is buried.

GORY GEORGIANS

The Georgian age (1714–1830) was a great time for building great houses. The 'Industrial Revolution' brought huge amounts of money to some people. Their mills and factories turned the poor into slaves and towns into soot-stained slums.

The rich didn't want to live in those towns. They wanted to escape to the clean country air.

The Georgian kings made many of these rich men into lords. But some of them could be lousy lords as well as brutal bosses.

33. LONGLEAT
Wiltshire, England

Thomas Thynne, 2nd Viscount of Weymouth (1710–1751) was famous for his filthy temper. His terrible tale is horrible ... but it happened. Probably. Oh, all right ... *possibly.*

IN 1733 THYNNE MARRIED LOVELY LOUISA CARTERET AND SHE MOVED IN TO LONGLEAT HOUSE

SOUNDS LIKE A SOPPY LOVE STORY, CAN YOU MAKE IT INTERESTING?

I COULD SWAP SOME OF THE WORDS AROUND...

GO ON THEN

Louisa loved the Longleat (1) mouse/house.

She also loved her old (2) toys/servants so she took them with her when she moved.

One (3) footballer/footman called James was devoted to her.

The Longleat servants were jealous of James because Louisa made him her (4) treacle-tart/favourite.

So one of them told Thynne the lie that the footman was after his (5) life/wife.

Thynne flew into a (6) high-flying-pig/rage.

He threw James down (7) in-the-dumps/the stairs.

James was buried in the cellar and Thynne told Louisa he had run (8) a bath/away.

Louisa was afraid James was a prisoner in a (9) pickle/room and ran around Longleat searching for him.

She grew ill and weak because she was expecting a (10) pizza delivery/baby.

How many did you score?

Answer:
The second word is always the correct one.

Louisa caught a chill and died. Now she haunts Longleat house as the 'Green Lady'.

A silly story? Would a lord murder a servant and bury his body under the cellar floor?

And the answer is … maybe. In the 1900s the owner of Longleat dug up the cellar to put in central heating. The skeleton of a man was found there … wearing the uniform of a footman from the 1730s.

The bones were stuffed in a shoebox and buried in the churchyard.

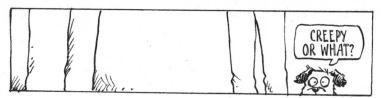

There now

Longleat is the home of the Marquis of Bath. The safari park outside is also home to over 500 animals, including giraffes, monkeys, rhinos, lions, tigers and wolves. The house and the park are open throughout the year.

34. FYVIE CASTLE
Aberdeenshire, Scotland

Ghostly Grey Lady

Gruesome great houses like Longleat make a habit of having skeletons hidden away. All those bones make the places spooky.

NOT NECESSARILY

In 1920 a skeleton was found in the wall at Fyvie Castle. Local people say it is the skeleton of Lady Meldrum who died in the 1200s. It is said she ASKED to be buried in the walls of a secret room in the Meldrum Tower.

Of course she haunted the place and can be seen as a moaning Grey Lady. What was she moaning about, we wonder?

WOE, WOE

WHO STUCK THAT AWFUL YELLOW WALLPAPER OVER MY GRAVE?

The skeleton was found hidden in the walls about a hundred years ago. It was then moved to the church and buried there, but the ghost was really upset. She started appearing and causing disasters. The lord had her skeleton stuck back in the wall and she calmed down again.

Another Green Lady

There is also a Green Lady at Fyvie. (It's nice to know the Grey Lady has company.)

She is said to be the ghost of Dame Lilias Drummond who married Lord Alexander Seton in the days of Queen Elizabeth I. The family needed sons to carry on the Seton name at Fyvie. Poor Lilias had five daughters.

To make it worse Lord Alexander Seton began flirting with Lilias's cousin, Grizel.

Then Lilias did a careless thing and died in 1601. There is a mixed up legend that says Lord Alexander starved Lilias to death so he could marry Grizel. (That's probably nonsense.)

Was Lord Alexander Seton upset, heartbroken and forlorn?

No. He married his wife's cousin and tried to live happily ever after. But Lilias came back to hang around outside their bedroom window. When they looked out of the window they knew it was Lilias. How?

a) She waved and said, 'Hello, I'm Lilias. Remember me?'

b) She carved her name in the stone windowsill, 'D LILIAS DRUMMOND'.

c) She begs and cries, 'Have you got a crust of bread? I'm famished.'

Answer (b)
Go to Fyvie Castle today and you can still see the
name scratched into the sill.
D LILIAS DRUMMOND

The weeping stones

Why did Lilias have five daughters but no sons? Because Fyvie
was cursed. An old Scottish prophet called Thomas the Rhymer
visited Fyvie. He said the stones of Preston Tower had been
stolen from an ancient burial site and until they were returned...

A BOY WILL NEVER BE BORN IN FYVIE AGAIN

(So, it seems that curse came true.)

There were three stolen stones, Tom said. They shouldn't
be moved ... they are weeping because they've been moved.
He even recited a rotten rhyme:

Fyvie, Fyvie, you'll never thrive
As long as there's three stones in you.
There's one in the oldest tower,
There's one in the lady's bower,
There's one in the water-gate.
And these three stones you'll never get.

The stones are supposed to stay wet when the other stones
around them are dry ... they stay dry when all around them
are wet.

Ghostly gathering

A phantom man in tartan can be seen near the castle wall. This may be the ghost of Andrew Lammie. He died of a broken heart after hearing of the death of his beloved Agnes who lived there.

The Fyvie Castle ghosts

Fyvie also has a room with a stain on the floor – a bloodstain that can never be washed out. They say a lady was locked away there. When gallant men came to rescue her they were chopped down and their corpses thrown out of the window. You can still see the stain and the window … but not the corpses.

There now

The castle is open to visitors at certain times of the year.

35. OLD HASTINGS HOUSE
East Sussex, England

John Collier was mayor of Hastings and owned Old Hastings House from 1735 to 1750. John had a great aim in life – he wanted to smash the smuggling gangs that infested the area.

Sussex and Kent were crawling with smugglers because it was just a short sail from there to France. John never gave up the fight ... yet a lot of people hated him. These people WANTED the smugglers to get away with their crimes ... even get away with murder.

Smashing smugglers

There's a sweet English poem about smugglers, with the cute chorus:

> *Five and twenty ponies, trotting through the dark –*
> *Brandy for the parson. 'Baccy for the clerk;*
> *Laces for a lady, letters for a spy,*
> *And watch the wall, my darling, while the gentlemen go by!*

The poem is supposed to be a mother talking to her little daughter. She's saying DON'T go blabbing to the soldiers about these smugglers because they're really nice chaps. Just turn away and ignore them.

Things like the 'baccy' (tobacco) and brandy came to England in ships and a tax had to be paid.

But if you landed the stuff secretly at night in a quiet spot then you could dodge the tax. Result? Cheap baccy and brandy.

The trouble is those smugglers were not 'gentlemen' … and most were not 'gentle' men. They were thugs.

In 1748 old William Galley, a tax collector, and David Chater, a customs officer, set off to go to court. They were going to tell a judge all about the Hawkhurst smuggling gang from Kent but they got lost.

They stopped for a drink, but picked a smugglers' inn. Terrible bad luck. Friends of the Hawkhurst gang met them. They…

* got the two men drunk
* tied their victims back to back then sat them on a horse
* whipped them both, then buried William Galley alive in a foxhole to die
* kept Chater prisoner in chains for three days then threw him down a nine-metre well
* piled stones down the well to make sure he was dead

Murder for the sake of cheap booze and fags? Gentlemen?

Six gentleman smugglers were hanged and their corpses sent around the south of England to hang in chains till they rotted. John Collier must have loved that.

Would you 'watch the wall'? Better not – the wall may be splashed with blood.

There now

Old Hastings House is a care home. John Collier's stables became The Stables Theatre.

Magical stones. Do you believe in them? A lot of Scots do. And the most magical of all is the Stone of Scone, from the Palace there. It's been a stolen stone (twice) and a history mystery.

SAY IT 'SCONE' TO RHYME WITH JUNE

NOT 'JOHN'

OR 'BONE'

Terrible tale

Around the year 850, Kenneth MacAlpin battled to make himself the first true king of all Scotland.

The great rivals of the Scots were the Picts. MacAlpin invited the Pict King Drostan, with all his chief warriors, to a feast with him at Scone Palace.

The Picts sat and guzzled food and drink. Suddenly the Scots pulled out the bolts that held the benches together. The Picts fell to the floor into a trap that held them by the legs.

The Scots massacred them. That's how to get rid of your rivals.

The stone throne mystery

The Scots believed that all their kings should be crowned while sitting on the 'Stone of Destiny' – a lump of red sandstone that weighs 152kg. They believe Saint Columba took it round Scotland to preach from.

In 1297 King Edward I of England decided to put a stop to this nonsense. He pinched the stone from the throne at Scone and carried it back to England. Edward had a special throne built over the stone and put it in Westminster Abbey in London. It stayed in England for 700 years. Or did it?

There's a story that the monks of the abbey near Scone knew what King Ed was up to and switched the stone for a fake before Edward got there. The real stone was carried to the Western Isles where it has remained to this day.

So 30 English kings and queens weren't crowned on the 'Stone of Destiny'. They were crowned on a lump of old rock and the Scots have had a seven-hundred-year laugh.

EVEN MY BAGPIPES ARE LAUGHING

AND THAT'S NOT SOMETHING YOU HEAR EVERY DAY

Nice story, but is it true?

Here's a clue. In 1328, Edward III (the thief's grandson) made peace with the Scots and he offered to return the Stone of Destiny to Scotland. The Scots didn't want it. Why not?

Maybe because they knew it was a fake?

Scone again

In 1950 some students called Ian Hamilton, Gavin Vernon, Kay Matheson and Alan Stuart, raided Westminster Abbey to steal the stone and take it back to Scotland. They weren't very good thieves but the London police were worse…

116

The police found out who had stolen the stone but the students were never arrested. The thieves got away with their crime and became heroes in Scotland.

There now

The ancient abbot's Scone Palace had been a Catholic abbey. A Protestant mob from Dundee flattened the ancient building in 1559.

Now you can see a newer palace built in 1808. The gardens and palace are open to the public.

In 1996 the Stone of Scone was taken back to Scotland, and you can see it in Edinburgh Castle.

37. BLAIR ATHOLL
Perth and Kinross, Scotland

The Georgian kings were from Germany. But there were rebels, known as Jacobites, who were mostly from Scotland. They wanted the old Stuarts back on the throne. Bonnie Prince Charlie led their Stuart rebellion – he was a hero in the Scottish Highlands and islands. Not so much in the Lowlands.

The last siege

300 of King George's troops set up camp in Blair Castle. Charlie's Highlanders camped outside and made sure no food got in. George's men began to starve.

The highlanders fired their cannons at the castle.

Their cannons were as pathetic as pea-shooters. The highlanders had a new idea…

The men in the castle had a better idea. They took ladles from the castle kitchens, scooped up the hot cannonballs and dropped them into barrels of cool liquid.

That's right. The English put the fires out with their pee.

The soldiers in the castle grew bored. They made a dummy of their general, Sir Andrew Agnew. They put a telescope in the dummy's hand and set it in a window to spy on the highlanders. The attackers blasted away at the window. Sir Andrew was furious.

The Scots decided to offer peace to the English in the castle. But they knew about Sir Andrew's bad temper. No one dared to take a message to him.

Then an unlikely hero stepped forward ... it was Molly, the barmaid from the inn at Blair.

Molly passed the message through a window, heard Sir Andrew's screams of rage and she ran for her life.

The siege went on two more weeks and food in the castle was low.

The trapped men sent out a messenger on horseback, asking George's army to come to their rescue. The soldier rode out ... the next thing the English saw was a Scotsman riding back on the messenger's horse.

They hadn't. The Highlanders saw the messenger and fired at him. He got such a shock he fell off the horse and the Scots captured it.

Soon after that the Highland attackers marched off. There was a great battle planned to the North and they were going to be part of it.

The last siege in Britain ended. The last battle began.

The last battle

Bonnie Prince Charlie. He wasn't very bonnie but he looked a proper Charlie when his tartan army was crushed at the Battle of Culloden.

When the Highlanders charged forward they were brilliantly brave and hopelessly lost. It was a massacre and it lasted barely three-quarters of an hour.

Culloden was not only the last battle to be fought on British soil. It was one of the most brutal. The Duke of Cumberland gave orders that there should be no prisoners taken. The wounded Scots who were left on the battlefield were murdered. There are even stories of Highland prisoners being burned alive.

There now

Blair Castle is open to the public.

38. LINLITHGOW PALACE
West Lothian, Scotland

The Duke of Cumberland, also known as 'The Butcher', butchered the Scots at Culloden then marched back home to England. On the way home he wrecked a few Scottish castles, palaces and great houses.

It seems like a spiteful thing to do. He wanted to leave a lesson to Scotland's rebels: 'You don't battle with the Butcher.'

One of the palaces he burned was Linlithgow – the place where the sad Mary, Queen of Scots had been born in 1542.

Before then Linlithgow had been a king's house in the 1100s. Then King Edward I of England invaded in the late 1200s.

EDWARD I TURNED LINLITHGOW INTO A FORTRESS

NO HE DIDN'T. HIS BUILDERS DID

SHE'S RIGHT, YOU KNOW

Yes, the rich didn't 'build' these gruesome great houses themselves … they didn't want to get their hands dirty. An old book tells of how Edward's orders were carried out…

In September 1302, 60 men and 140 women helped dig the ditches.

The men were paid 2 pence and the women 1 pence each day. A hundred foot soldiers were still working on the castle in November and work carried on till the Summer of 1303.

So the women did the same work as the men but were paid half as much.

SOME THINGS DON'T CHANGE

Bonnie Prince Charlie had visited Linlithgow on his rebel march but he didn't stay there. One report says the fountains were turned on for him and they flowed with wine. After Culloden they were filled with ashes.

Mary, Queen of Scots does NOT haunt this castle … but her Mum, Mary of Guise, DOES. She died in Edinburgh Castle … some say Elizabeth I of England had her poisoned.

Mary of Guise's body was wrapped in lead (so it didn't rot and smell) and was taken back to her home in France.

WE SAW THE GHOST OF MARY OF GUISE

AND IT DIDN'T SMELL

There now
The palace is open to visitors.

39. HAREWOOD HOUSE
West Yorkshire, England

The sooty factories made fortunes for the lucky factory owners. They built their great houses from the sweat of the workers. But some great Georgian houses were built with the riches from the slave trade.

Between 1773 and 1787 Edwin Lascelles got himself more than 27,000 acres and 2,947 slaves in the West Indies. They were worth £293,000 (about £28.3 million today). His home, Harewood House, was built using his father's slave money when Edwin was just a young man starting out in the trade.

Slavery was banned in 1833. By then Henry Lascelles, 2nd Earl of Harewood, owned Harewood House. But the slave owners were paid to give up their slaves. Henry got nearly £2 million. STILL the slavers weren't happy. Henry whinged...

I am a sufferer; but some of my friends suffer more. They have nothing but their slave estates to make them money.

I'M DOWN TO MY LAST BILLION

Poor slave owners. It was worse for the slaves.

Suffering slaves

Olaudah Equiano was captured when he was a child and sold as a slave. Olaudah said…

The grown-ups of our village used to go off to work in the fields. The children then gathered together to play. But, whenever we played we always sent someone up a tree to watch out for slave dealers. This was the time when slave dealers rushed into the village, snatched as many children as they could, and carried them off to the coast. Then they were sold as slaves.

Imagine that. You go to play in your local park – before you know it a gang has picked you up and sold you. You'd never see your home or your family again. Cruel.

Sardine slaves

Slaves were worth a lot of money but the traders didn't take very good care of them. Many died, packed like sardines in a tin into dark, stinking rooms below the decks of the ships. The sailors did wash them down every day – probably a bucket of sea water thrown over the slave.

A young slave described the journey of between forty and seventy days across the Atlantic Ocean…

The stench and the heat was dreadful. The crowding meant you hardly had room to turn over. The chains rubbed some Africans raw. The filth was made worse by the lavatory bucket and many small children fell into it. One day two of my countrymen were allowed on deck. They were chained together and decided they would rather have death than such a life of misery. They jumped into the sea.

Did you know?

While the slaves were eating vegetable-mush the slave-traders back in Britain had more food than they knew what to do with. In 1769 slave trader William Beckford had a feast. 600 dishes were served on golden plates. It cost £10,000.

There now

Harewood House is open to the public at certain times of the year.

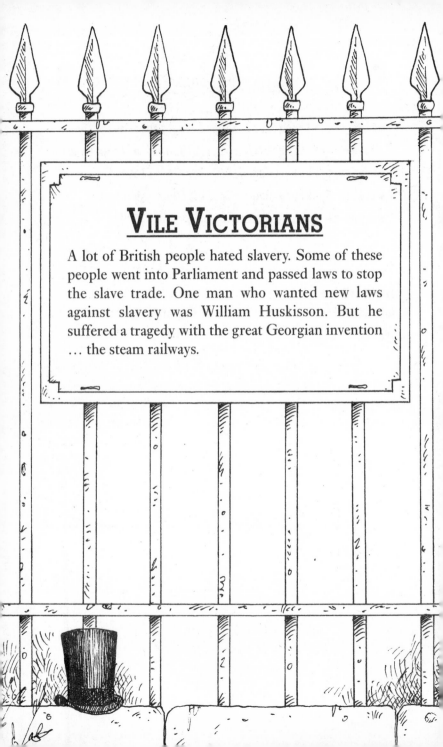

VILE VICTORIANS

A lot of British people hated slavery. Some of these people went into Parliament and passed laws to stop the slave trade. One man who wanted new laws against slavery was William Huskisson. But he suffered a tragedy with the great Georgian invention … the steam railways.

40. BIRTSMORTON COURT
Worcestershire, England

In 1830, when Victoria was just a princess, the world's first passenger railway opened. It ran from Manchester to Liverpool.

It was a great day for William Huskisson, the MP for Liverpool. It was also his last day.

Huskisson was born at Birtsmorton Court and grew up there. There was a house there in Norman times. There is a moat around it so it was safe from attack even though it wasn't a castle.

NEVER MIND, A HOUSE WITH A MOAT DOES HAVE IT'S ADVANTAGES

Huskisson horror

William Huskisson was a guest when the first passenger trains ran from Liverpool to Manchester. There were two tracks, side by side, and the special trains ran on both tracks. The Prime Minister, Arthur Wellesley, 1st Duke of Wellington, was on one track. William Huskisson's train on the other.

A witness described Huskisson's sad death:

The 'Northumbrian' locomotive pulled a carriage that carried the Duke of Wellington. When it stopped William Huskisson MP stepped down onto the other track to greet him.

The train pulled by 'Rocket' was seen rapidly coming up on that other track. The Duke of Wellington stretched out to shake the hand of Huskisson.

A hurried, friendly grasp was given and, before it was loosed, there was a general cry of 'Get in. Get in.'

Mr Huskisson, flustered, attempted to get around the open door but in so doing was struck down by the 'Rocket'.

His first words on being raised were, 'I have met my death.'

Huskisson's leg was mangled. He was put in a carriage on the duke's train. They raced to get him to hospital but he died later that night.

Did you know?

❀ There is a moat around Birtsmorton Court.
There are over 5,000 great houses with moats
in Britain. Only around 30 still have water in
them. The moat at Birtsmorton would have been
full of fish. But they weren't there to look
pretty (like a goldfish pond). They were there
to be eaten in the great house's kitchen.

❀ A second moat runs around a cattle pen and the
cows were shut in there every night. The water
would save the cattle from being attacked by
wild boars.

❀ Henry VIII's minister, Cardinal Wolsey, often
went to Birtsmorton. An old story says he sat
beneath a tree in the garden and had a vision
– he saw his own execution. The tree is known
as the Wolsey Tree. Yet Wolsey WASN'T executed.
Henry ordered him to go to the Tower of London
but Wolsey died before he got there.

There now

Birtsmorton Court is a private house but
open to the public.

41. GAD'S HILL PLACE
Kent, England

William Huskisson may have been the first victim of the railways but he wasn't the last.

The man who wrote horrible history stories back in the days of Queen Victoria was Charles Dickens. Dickens ended his days in Gad's Hill Place.

He wrote popular stories, like *A Christmas Carol* and *Oliver Twist*. Even though they were 'stories' there was a lot of truth in them.

He saw some dreadful things in putrid places. He changed the names of the people and places and told the stories. Stories like Nicholas Nickelby. The book looks at a savage school he calls Dotheboys Hall and a twisted teacher he calls Wackford Squeers.

The school was really Bowes Academy in County Durham and the teacher was William Shaw. Pupils were so badly treated some went blind and others died.

AT LEAST THEY DIDN'T HAVE SATS IN DICKENS' DAY

AND YOU THINK *YOUR* SCHOOL IS BAD?

Dickens told the tale in Nicholas Nickelby…

The little boy screwed a couple of knuckles into each of his eyes and began to cry, wherefore Mr Squeers knocked him off the trunk with a blow on one side of the face, and knocked him on again with a blow on the other.

'Wait till I get you down into Yorkshire, my young gentleman,' said Mr Squeers, 'and then I'll give you the rest.'

Nicholas Nickelby arrived at the school and made friends with the dim and frightened Smike. When Squeers started to whip Smike then Nicholas attacked Squeers…

Nicholas sprang upon him, wrested the weapon from his hand, and pinning him by the throat, beat the ruffian till he roared for mercy.

Dickens had met the head teacher, William Shaw, in the real Bowes School and said he was a 'scoundrel'.

Dickens then went to the graveyard of the church next to Bowes School. He said...

The first gravestone I stumbled on that dreary winter afternoon was placed above the grave of a boy, eighteen long years old, who had died suddenly ... died at that wretched school. I think his ghost put Smike into my head, upon the spot.

Bowes Academy – and a lot of other cruel schools – were forced to close down after Dickens wrote about them.

Dickens grew rich from his writing and bought Gad's Hill Place. But he didn't enjoy a long and happy life there.

Terrible tale

The staplehurst rail crash was a railway accident in Kent, England. Ten passengers died and fifty more were injured.

Charles Dickens was on board with his mistress, Nell Ternan, and her mother. The writer helped many of the injured and saw some of them die. But the shock was terrible. He wrote fewer books after the accident. He said:

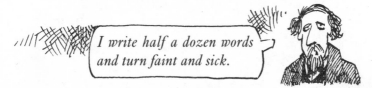

I write half a dozen words and turn faint and sick.

The crash bothered him for the rest of his life. It made him ill and afraid of trains. The accident happened in 1865 on 9 June. Charles Dickens died five years later in 1870 … on the same day, 9 June.

Did the shock of the crash make his life shorter?

There now

Charles Dickens first saw Gad's Hill Place in 1821, when he was nine years old. His father John Dickens told Charles that if he worked hard enough, one day he would own it. 35 years later he did.

In 1924 the house became Gad's Hill School, which it still is. Like most schools today it is not quite so bad as Dotheboys Hall and the teachers aren't quite so cruel as William Shaw.

Bowes Academy in Durham has now turned into flats. But the church is still there with the gravestone of the boy that Dickens turned into poor Smike. William Shaw is also buried there.

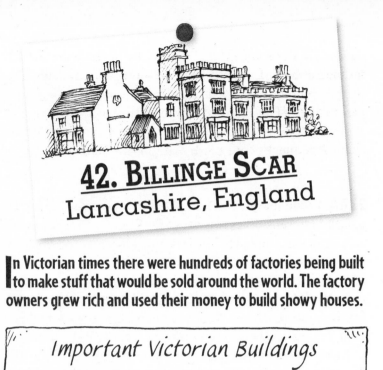

42. BILLINGE SCAR
Lancashire, England

In Victorian times there were hundreds of factories being built to make stuff that would be sold around the world. The factory owners grew rich and used their money to build showy houses.

Important Victorian Buildings

Busy factory   Grand mansion   Stinking hovel

In 1876 Daniel Thwaites turned Billinge Scar, near Blackburn, from a small home into a great house. It was built to look like a Tudor mansion.

Dan then moved and sold the house to William Birtwhistle, a cotton manufacturer. Will's factories used weaving machines called looms to make cloth. It's said he owned more looms than any other person in the world.

These looms, and others before them, were noisy and

dangerous. But someone had to work them and make money for their owners. Those workers had short and miserable lives.

Mill misery facts

1. Workers were fined if they were caught whistling or singing as they worked.

2. They would also be fined if they were caught talking to someone from another row of workers.

3. Work started at 6 a.m. but there was no time for breakfast till 8 a.m. There was an hour break for lunch and 20 minutes for tea.

4. Some managers altered the clock so workers would be late for work and the manager could cut their wages.

5. In the early days, parents would take little children to work with them. These kids were used as free workers for the owners.

6. When Victoria came to the throne in 1837, children as young as five still worked in the mills. New laws changed that. By 1874 they had to be ten to work in a factory.

7. Small children called 'scavengers' were used for cleaning out looms while the machines were running. Mill machines could chop off careless fingers, hands or arms. The wounds could get infected and kill the child.

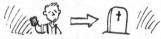

8. In 1833 a new law said children under 13 could 'only' work 48 hours a week.

9. In the Blackburn mills workers breathed air full of dust, oil and soot. Young people were lucky to live to 17.

10. Ribbon–making was one of the most dangerous jobs.

A report said:

> *Three hundred boys were turning hand looms. The endless whirl had a bad effect on their heads and stomachs. The little turners often suffered brain and spine damage and some died of it. In one mill there were six deaths and 60 serious accidents in just four years.*

The mill owners made their money and built their great houses. The workers lived in slums.

There now
Billinge Scar was knocked down in 1947. Only the coach house is still there.

43. BUCKINGHAM PALACE
London, England

Queen Victoria ruled over the British Empire. Many of her people brought fortunes back from around the world and used the wealth to build great houses with dozens of rooms and dozens of servants. They weren't all happy places. They weren't all comfortable. Not even Victoria's new home ... Buckingham Palace.

Fascinating facts

❀ When the palace was built it was called Buckingham House.

❀ It was built for the Duke of Buckingham in 1703.

❀ Buckingham House was bought by King George III in 1761 as a home for Queen Charlotte while he stayed in St James's Palace.

❀ It then became known as 'The Queen's House'.

❀ 14 of Charlotte's 15 children were born there.

❀ During the 1800s it was patched up and made bigger.

🌼 Queen Victoria was the first Brit ruler to move into Buckingham Palace ... and it was a real mess.

🌼 The chimneys smoked all the time.

🌼 The walls were damp.

🌼 Victoria's staff were lazy and the palace was dirty.

🌼 The stench of rotten food drifted up from the cellar.

Lousy land

William the Conqueror had lived in a house on that spot. But it had been a marsh so the houses built there were usually damp. William gave the great house away – who can blame him.

The man who took over then gave it away to some monks.

The village in that place was called Eye Cross.

Eye Cross House rotted so King James I used the land to rear silkworms, then sold the rest.

Lord Goring bought the land and built a fine house there ... but it burned down.

Did you know?

An odd Victorian lad known as 'The Boy Jones' kept breaking in to the palace. The first time he was caught with a pair of Queen Vic's knickers stuffed inside his jacket.

He was caught twice more, once having a nap on her couch, then having a snack in her kitchens.

The Boy Jones was sent to serve in the navy and ended up as the Town Crier of Perth in Australia. But he got drunk one night, fell off the Mitchell River bridge and landed on his head. Splat. Dead.

There now

The ruler of the UK still lives there. Some rooms are open to the public on certain days of the year.

44. CASTELL COCH
Glamorgan, Wales

The Marquess of Bute was rich. As the Welsh miners sweated underground to dig the coal the Marquess had Castell Coch (Red Castle) built as a spare home for when he fancied a change.

Castell Coch was built to look like a castle from the Middle Ages. It really was built on the spot where an ancient castle stood. And that led to some strange stories.

If the castle had a Horrible Histories guide to show people around they may have told visitors the gruesome stuff.

THE RED CASTLE — JUST OUTSIDE CARDIFF. A FAIRYTALE CASTLE. OPEN TO THE PUBLIC MOST DAYS OF THE YEAR

HAVE YOU FINISHED? OUR VISITORS WANT TO HEAR THE HORRIBLE HISTORY

There now

Castell Coch is open to the public at certain times of the year.

45. EUSTON HALL
Suffolk, England

Queen Victoria's British Empire invaded countries all around the world.

The men who risked their lives over and over again were the sailors. One great sailor was Robert FitzRoy (1805–1865). He discovered new ways to tell what the weather would be like – very important if you are setting sail. FitzRoy invented the weather word we all use today – 'forecast'.

The FitzRoy family lived at Euston Hall. The first FitzRoy was Henry and his dad was King Charles II. Cheerful Charlie arranged a marriage for Henry to marry the rich Isabella. The wedding took place when she was old enough. She was 12. You can still get married at Euston Hall … but you have to be over 16 now … not 12.

PHEW

Robert FitzRoy became a famous FitzRoy for starting one of the Empire's strangest wars...

The Flagstaff War

The Brit sailors 'discovered' New Zealand and settled there. They made peace with the natives then got the natives to sign over the land to Queen Victoria. The Brits gave the Maoris booze and guns – the Maoris gave the Brits New Zealand.

Five hundred Maori chiefs agreed to the deal. Robert FitzRoy was made governor over the invaders and the Maori natives.

One disagreed. That rebel was called Hone Heke Pokai. He couldn't attack Queen Victoria but he COULD attack the sign of her power – the British flag that flew from Flagstaff Hill. FitzRoy arrived with soldiers to guard the flagstaff.

If Governor FitzRoy had written a diary of 1844 and 1845 then some of the entries may have looked like this:

<u>10 January 1845</u>

Our new flag pole stood proudly on Flagstaff Hill – until this morning. Some Maoris sneaked up and chopped it down – again. It's guarded by 170 soldiers sent from Australia. We can't let sneaky Heke get away with it. Victoria's flag shall fly. The new flagstaff will be covered with iron.

18 January 1845

New flag pole chopped down a third time. It was guarded by Maoris. This is beyond a joke. Britannia rules the waves, and Britons never, never, never shall have their flags flattened. I have a marvellous plan to nobble the natives. I am taking a huge old ship's mast – thick as a tree trunk. The Maoris can attack it, but it will take them so long to chop down we'll have the army there to stop them. The post is defended by a small fort. That's the end of horrible Heke's game.

11 March 1845

Disaster. The flag pole is down. The men at the fort were digging ditches when Heke's men leapt on them and massacred them with their knives and coral-studded clubs. Maoris also attacked the town and set it on fire. The biggest explosion was in the gunpowder dump – not caused by the Maoris, but by a British workman with a careless spark from his pipe. (I always thought smoking was bad for your health.)

We British retreated to the safety of a warship – six men who went back for their valuables were hacked down. Final score, 19 British settlers dead and 29 wounded.

All for the sake of a flag.

BUT IT DOESN'T HAVE A FLAGPOLE

Governor FitzRoy returned to England while the war against the Maoris raged on for another year.

And that flag? Heke died of a disease in 1850, six years after he started flattening flagpoles – but while he lived that flagpole was never raised again.

Robert FitzRoy returned to England but lost all his money. In 1865 he killed himself.

So who won? No one. Who lost? As usual, everyone.

There now

Robert FitzRoy's family home, Euston Hall, is open to the public on certain dates throughout the year.

46. Alnwick Castle
Northumberland, England

Alnwick Castle was built as a border fortress. The Scots liked to march down and try to bash it about. It began to fall into ruin in the 1600s then was repaired and made into a comfy house for the Dukes of Northumberland.

CAN WE NOT BASH IT ABOUT ANY MORE?

SCOTLAND

Victorian times were hard for the workers but they did have fun on one day each year … Shrove Tuesday (or Pancake Day). That's when they played…

Scoring the Hales

This is a sort of football match. If you like a few laughs, don't mind a few broken arms and legs, and you are a strong swimmer then you can try it for yourself.

SCORING THE HALES

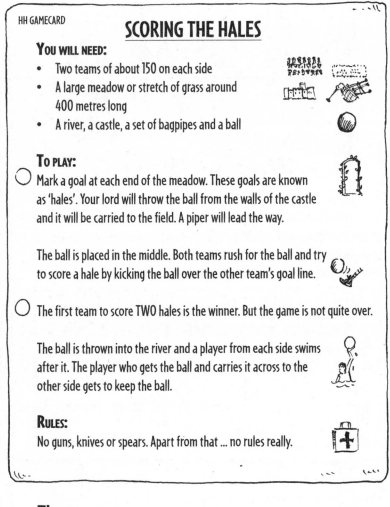

YOU WILL NEED:

- Two teams of about 150 on each side
- A large meadow or stretch of grass around 400 metres long
- A river, a castle, a set of bagpipes and a ball

TO PLAY:

Mark a goal at each end of the meadow. These goals are known as 'hales'. Your lord will throw the ball from the walls of the castle and it will be carried to the field. A piper will lead the way.

The ball is placed in the middle. Both teams rush for the ball and try to score a hale by kicking the ball over the other team's goal line.

The first team to score TWO hales is the winner. But the game is not quite over.

The ball is thrown into the river and a player from each side swims after it. The player who gets the ball and carries it across to the other side gets to keep the ball.

RULES:

No guns, knives or spears. Apart from that ... no rules really.

There now

Alnwick Castle is open to the public for most of the year.

Scoring the Hales is still played in the fields beside Alnwick Castle every Shrove Tuesday.

WOEFUL WARS

The age of Victoria was cruel with sweaty factories
and little boys sent up chimneys. Victoria died in 1901
and it was a new century, a new age. A worse age was
coming.

There were two massive wars in the last century.
The First World War fought from 1914 to 1918 and
the Second World War from 1939 to 1945.

Many great houses were used to help the war –
they became hospitals for wounded soldiers or schools
for children from bombed cities. Some were turned
into homes for training spies or breaking enemy
codes. Others were useful for spying on the enemy.

47. TRENT PARK
Greater London, England

Richard Jebb was a doctor. In 1777 he went to Trento in Italy and saved the life of King George III's little brother, Prince William.

JEBB YOU ARE A REALLY HOT DOC. I AM GOING TO LET YOU LIVE IN AN OLD HUNTING PARK

YOU'RE NOT SO MAD AS THEY SAY YOU ARE

Jebb built a house there and called it Trent Park after the place in Italy.

Jebb wasn't so lucky with princesses. Ten years after saving Prince William he was sent to cure two princesses. He caught a fever…

YOU REALLY ARE A HOT DOCTOR

Jebb died. New owners added to Jebb's house to make the mansion you can see today. But in 1939 the army found a new use for it.

I spy with my little ear

When enemy aircraft were shot down over England, the airmen would become prisoners of war … if they lived. They weren't usually sent straight to a prison camp but to one of three great English houses. Trent Park was one, Latimer House and Wilton Park the others.

The rooms at these great houses had been fitted with hidden microphones. British spies listened to the German airmen as they chatted and gave away secrets. The spies learned a lot about enemy aircraft …

Later in the war German army officers were held at Trent Park – 60 generals stayed there. They were given fine food and whisky to loosen their tongues. They were allowed to walk around the park. But the British spies had hung microphones from trees to catch what they were chatting about. That must have confused the squirrels.

General von Thoma talked about German V1 and V2 rocket bombs that were being built in Germany. The Trent Park spies told the Royal Air Force who sent bombers to Germany to destroy the rocket factories. Those spy microphones must have saved many lives.

The spies heard some real horror stories when the Germans talked about their prisoner of war camps where men, women and children were massacred. One general told a story of meeting a Nazi executioner…

The Nazi told me I could visit his camp to film one of the shootings. He said, 'These people are always shot in the morning. But we still have a few left over, and we could always shoot some in the afternoon if you like.'

That's the most horrible history of all.

There now

Trent Park became a college for teachers when the war ended. The house closed in 2014 but the park is still open.

48. ARISAIG HOUSE
Inverness-shire, Scotland

In 1939 Britain went to war with Adolf Hitler. Hitler's armies had invaded France. British soldiers landed in France but were driven back.

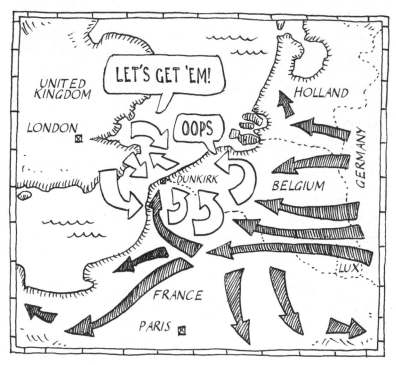

If the British Army couldn't defeat the Germans then maybe the French people could 'resist'? So a secret group of French people formed the 'Resistance'. They laid bombs in German army camps and their army trains, they assassinated German leaders and helped airmen to escape back to Britain to fly again. In 1940 the British war leader was Winston Churchill and he had an idea. Let's help the Resistance by sending secret agents and spies and weapons to France to help the French fighters.

Let us set Europe ablaze.

He set up the 'Special Operations Executive' – or SOE for short.

But the secret army needed to be trained and they had to do it in secret. Where could Churchill's SOE find houses with walls around them to keep out spying eyes? The great houses of Britain, of course. The British Army took over dozens of them. The SOE agents even made a joke about it…

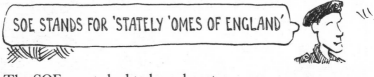

SOE STANDS FOR 'STATELY 'OMES OF ENGLAND'

The SOE agents had to learn how to…

❀ make false passports and papers
❀ fire guns and make bombs and booby-traps
❀ read maps and learn secret codes
❀ work wireless sets, spy on German troops and report back to Britain
❀ parachute, so they could be dropped and land in France

They had to learn all about France, what to wear, how to speak and how to live.

Arisaig House in Scotland was taken over by the SOE. Agents would learn how to fight like commandoes ... fighting alone or in small groups to attack then disappear into the countryside.

People who lived around Arisaig had to keep away from Arisaig House. They didn't want German spies spying on the British spies. The SOE had guards to check everyone who wanted to go near the house.

They failed.

One day a hay cart arrived at Arisaig House.

157

A German spy?

No a 15-year-old boy who was just being nosy.

The army learned a lesson. They had to be much more careful. If a boy could get into Arisaig then a German spy could. The SOE guards made sure it couldn't happen again.

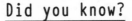

Did you know?

Arisaig House was used to train some of the most deadly assassins of the Second World War. In May 1942 Czech freedom fighters, trained at Arisaig, assassinated top Nazi, Reinhard Heydrich. It was the only Brit assassin plot that worked.

But the revenge of the Nazis for that assassination was terrible…

A newspaper of the time may have reported it like this:

CZECHOSLOVAKIA TODAY

11 June 1942   Prague Edition 2 Karona

MASSACRE
AT LIDICE

Hitler's hangman, Reinhard Heydrich, was killed by a freedom fighter's bomb in the Czech capital of Prague a week ago. Yesterday the German SS exacted their revenge.

They rounded up the inhabitants of Lidice and shot 173 men. Several women were shot while trying to escape and the rest were transported to Ravensbrück concentration camp. The children who could be 'Germanized' were given new names and sent to Germany to be raised by German families.

There now
Arisaig House is now a hotel.

49. BEAULIEU PALACE HOUSE
Hampshire, England

Beaulieu started life as a monastery. There is an old legend that said King John gave the money for the building. The story of how this came about is probably just a myth. The monastery was built for the Cistercians – the White Monks.

THE WHITE MONKS HAD UPSET KING JOHN

THOSE MONKS IN WHITE ARE A RIGHT SIGHT. I MIGHT FIGHT AND SMITE LIKE A KNIGHT

THE ABBOTS FROM THE WHITE-MONK MONASTERIES CAME TO PLEAD WITH JOHN

HE CALLED FOR HIS HORSE AND TRAMPLED THE ABBOTS INTO THE GROUND

NEVER SEEN A CRUELLER RULER

YOU'RE SUNK MONK

YOU SHOULD HAVE FLED

INSTEAD WE'RE DEAD

After the dissolution, when the monastery had been closed, the king's officers entered the abbey and found 32 criminals hiding there. Thomas Jeynes was a murderer and he was given a pardon.

The gatehouse of the Beaulieu was built up to be a fine country house.

In the Second World War the SOE used Beaulieu as a 'finishing school' for agents ... the last lessons before they were sent off to land in France. They were given their spy tools.

Spies in France could carry lots of useful things hidden in their luggage. If they were stopped, they would look like a simple traveller. Can you find where the secrets are hidden?

Get six out of six and you live. Any less and you will be executed ... probably.

This object hides ...	this secret
1. A tube of toothpaste	A. A miniature film
2. A tie	B. Money
3. A door key	C. A rubber balloon with a message
4. A bar of soap	D. Maps
5. A hairbrush	E. A secret code printed on silk
6. A pocket chess set	F. A message printed on silk

Answers:
1) A tube of toothpaste hides (C) A rubber balloon with a message
2) A tie hides (E) A secret code printed on silk
3) A door key hides (A) A miniature film
4) a bar of soap hides (F) A message printed on silk
5) a hairbrush hides (B) Money
6) a pocket chess set hides (D) Maps

There now

Beaulieu Palace House is home to the current Lord and Lady Montagu, but parts of the house and gardens are open daily to the public. It includes the National Motor Museum and a Secret Army Exhibition.

50. ASTON HOUSE
Stevenage, England

The SOE used Aston House to build and test secret weapons.

A 'Bailey Bridge' was invented there – a quick way to cross a river if the enemy had wrecked the old bridges. The model Bailey Bridge was made by Sir Robin Bailey using lollipop sticks, balsa wood and a lot of glue.

Some popular SOE gadgets were invented here. These were…

The Time Pencil
❀ This was a switch that set off a bomb. It was about the size of a pencil and looked harmless. All the spy had to do was set it to explode any time between 10 minutes or 24 hours … then run. There were about 12 million made from this Aston House invention.

🌸 The spies were allowed to test them on real targets in Britain. It sometimes went wrong. The spies were told they could blow up a railway track at the side of the main line … they blew up the main line instead. Doh.

🌸 A Time Pencil was put in a briefcase full of explosives and set to go off under the table where German leader Adolf Hitler was sitting. It worked fine, but the case had been moved behind the thick leg of the table. Hitler wasn't hurt … but his trousers were blown off.

The Limpet Mine
🌸 This bomb was made with a strong magnet.

🌸 A diver could swim below an enemy ship and the magnet would make it stick to the ship.

🌸 A Time Pencil would then set the bomb off once the diver was safely away.

There now
Only the Coach House and garden walls are still there, opposite the church. The house was flattened by Stevenage Development Corporation. They used the rooms in Aston House to plan Stevenage New Town … then knocked it down. Maybe they blew it up with a Time Pencil?

It has been said of Bristol and Liverpool that…

> *'Every brick in this miserable town was cemented with the blood of a slave.'*

Not real blood of course. It just means great towns were built from the money made from the slave trade.

Great houses were built from slave money too. In fact most great houses were built by rich people from the harsh work the poor suffered.

So you could look at the great houses and say…

> *'Every brick in this miserable house was cemented with the blood of the poor.'*

There are still hundreds of great houses around Britain. They look wonderful. But they were only great for the rich. And when you look at the stories you can see not even the rich were all that happy in them.

THIS GREAT HOUSE HAS SEEN SOME TERRIBLE TIMES

GRUESOME, IN FACT

GIFT SHOP →

INDEX

Also available

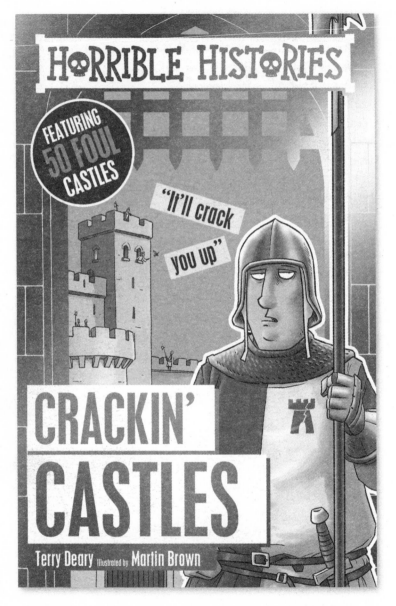

HORRIBLE HISTORIES

FEATURING 50 FOUL CASTLES

"It'll crack you up"

CRACKIN' CASTLES

Terry Deary Illustrated by Martin Brown

HORRIBLE HISTORIES

TOP 50 KINGS & QUEENS

ALFRED THE GREAT

HENRY VIII

VICTORIA

GOD SAVE OUR GRACIOUS ME

TERRY DEARY Illustrated by **MARTIN BROWN**

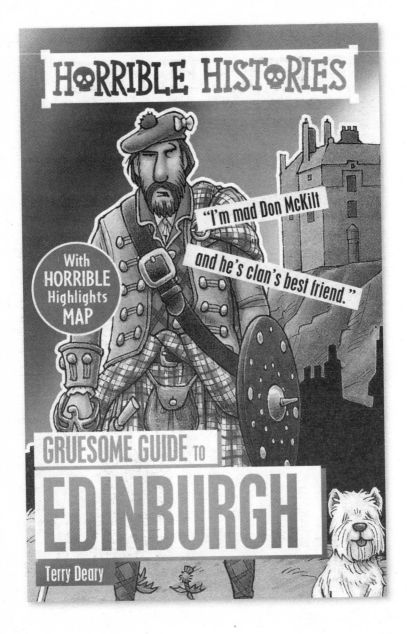

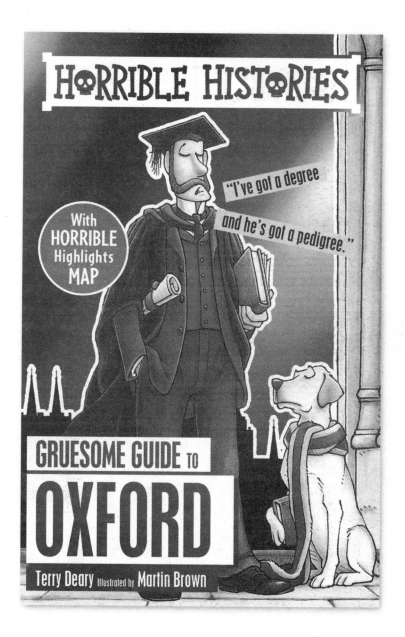

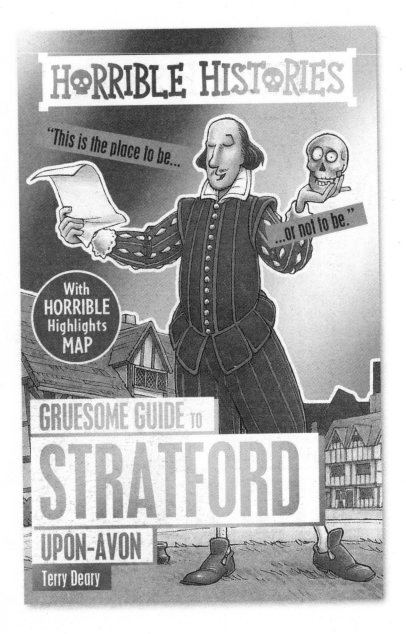

HORRIBLE HISTORIES

"GRRR!"

With
HORRIBLE
Highlights
MAP

GRUESOME GUIDE TO

YORK

Terry Deary

HORRIBLE HISTORIES

"Alive

alive

With HORRIBLE Highlights MAP

oh!"

GRUESOME GUIDE TO DUBLIN

Terry Deary

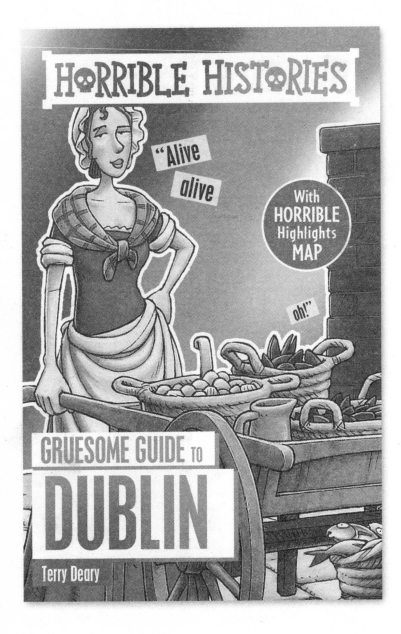